East Encounters West

STUDIES IN MIDDLE EASTERN HISTORY

Bernard Lewis, Itamar Rabinovich, and Roger Savory,
General Editors

Israel Gershoni and James P. Jankowski
EGYPT, ISLAM, AND THE ARABS
The Search for Egyptian Nationhood, 1900–1930

Ami Ayalon
LANGUAGE AND CHANGE
IN THE ARAB MIDDLE EAST

Fatma Müge Göçek
EAST ENCOUNTERS WEST
France and the Ottoman Empire
in the Eighteenth Century

Other Volumes Are in Preparation

EAST
ENCOUNTERS
WEST

*France and the Ottoman Empire
in the Eighteenth Century*

FATMA MÜGE GÖÇEK

New York   Oxford
OXFORD UNIVERSITY PRESS
*In cooperation with
The Institute of Turkish Studies, Inc.,
Washington, D.C.*
1987

Mw

Oxford University Press

Oxford   New York   Toronto
Delhi   Bombay   Calcutta   Madras   Karachi
Petaling Jaya   Singapore   Hong Kong   Tokyo
Nairobi   Dar es Salaam   Cape Town
Melbourne   Auckland

and associated companies in
Beirut   Berlin   Ibadan   Nicosia

Published by Oxford University Press, Inc.,
200 Madison Avenue, New York, New York 10016

Oxford is a registered trademark of Oxford University Press

Library of Congress Cataloging-in-Publication Data
Göçek, Fatma Müge.
East encounters West.
(Studies in Middle Eastern history)
Bibliography: p.   Includes index.
1. Turkey—Civilization—French influences. 2. Turkey—Civilization—
Occidental influences. 3. Turkey—Diplomatic and consular service—
France—History—18th century. I. Title.
II. Series: Studies in Middle Eastern history (New York, N.Y.)
DR432.G57   1987   956.1′01   86-23727
ISBN 0-19-504826-1

1 3 5 7 9 8 6 4 2

Printed in the United States of America

2-19-88

To my parents
Gülsen and Muzaffer Göçek,
with gratitude

PREFACE

Books evolve from the experiences of their authors. I can trace the idea for this book to my undergraduate years in Turkey during the 1970s when that country was trying to come to terms with social unrest. This unrest alerted me to the tension between the Eastern and Western civilizations in Turkey and as I explored this tension and tried to get to its roots, I found myself absorbed more and more in Ottoman history. Using an Ottoman embassy account to Paris in 1720–1721 as my starting point, I tried to understand the process by which the West influenced the Ottoman Empire throughout the eighteenth century.

My primary scholarly debt is to Bernard Lewis. Had it not been for his constant attentiveness to my work, his thorough critique, and his continuous support and encouragement, I would not have been able to develop this work into a book. I am also indebted, for their invaluable comments on earlier versions of this book, to Halil İnalcık, Heath Lowry, Gilles Veinstein on Ottoman history, Said Arjomand, Judith Herrin, Charles Issawi on historical analysis, Suzanne Keller, Robert Leibman, and Gilbert Rozman on social analysis, and Robert Palmer on French history. I would also like to thank Amy Singer who gave the manuscript a thorough reading.

I must express my appreciation to the students and teachers of the Near Eastern Studies and Sociology Departments of Princeton University from whose questions and comments I derived much benefit. I also learned from the comments I received during the two talks I gave on the Ottoman embassy account, one at the Third International Congress of the Social and Economic History of Turkey at Princeton in 1983, and the other at the Sadberk Hanım Müzesi in Istanbul in 1985. Needless to say, although all those from whom I have benefited account for much that is valuable in this book, I alone am responsible for any of its shortcomings.

Most of the illustrations in the book are from the Topkapı Museum Library; I would like to thank the Library director Filiz Çağman who was most supportive during my research in Istanbul. The Bibliothèque Nationale, especially Mileva Božič, and the French museums were most cooperative in providing the French illustrations.

Finally, I owe an immeasurable debt of thanks to my husband Charles Hammerslough who helped me type, read my chapters, and was there when I needed him.

Princeton   F.M.G.
October 1986

CONTENTS

APPENDIXES

ILLUSTRATIONS

NOTE ON TRANSCRIPTION
AND PRONUNCIATION

I have used modern Turkish spelling for the transcription of Ottoman words. The pronunciation of the following Turkish letters may be unfamiliar to the reader:

c	*j,* as in *j*ade
ç	*ch,* as in *ch*in
ğ	lengthens preceding vowel
ı	as the *o* in freed*o*m, or the *e* in wom*e*n
j	*zh,* as in vi*si*on
ö	French *eu,* as in d*eu*x
ş	*sh,* as in *sh*ade
ü	French *u,* as in d*u*rée

I

Interaction Between Two Societies Through an Embassy

Introduction

The eighteenth century marked the culmination of a rapid transformation in the West.[1] The scientific revolution, the discoveries of new lands and the resulting flow of wealth into Europe, the Enlightenment, and the increased communication among European states had altered Western societies. During this period, the West began to appear a monolithic power to non-Western societies. The encounters between these traditional societies and the West provide new insights into cultural differences between societies, and into the nature of cultural transmission and cultural diffusion. This book explores one response of traditional non-Western societies to the rising West through the case of the Ottoman Empire.

Western influence in Ottoman society emerged through a long process; the Western impact in the eighteenth century was transformed into Western influence as it diffused into Ottoman society. In previous centuries, the Ottoman Empire had encountered primarily the armies, navies, and merchants of the West, and had selected a few Western innovations for application in Ottoman society. During the eighteenth century, however, the Ottoman Empire had to face a different West; Western innovations now abounded: in military, navigational, and commercial techniques. This profusion of Western innovations upset the Ottoman control over the innovations that were allowed to enter Ottoman society; more and more entered and changed that society. By the end of the nineteenth century, this change became structurally visible as Western educational and administrative institutions such as schools and ministries were established in the Ottoman Empire.

In previous centuries, the Ottoman diplomatic contact with Europe had been limited; the Ottomans had no permanent representation in Europe while Europeans had representatives in the Ottoman Empire continuously. The contact between the Ottoman Empire and Europe was established in one direction, from Europe to the Ottoman Empire. As long as the Ottomans maintained their military superiority over Europe, this directionality did not create any problems for the Ottoman Empire. During the sixteenth and seventeenth

3

centuries, however, with the increasing consolidation of military power, material wealth, and scientific progress among the European states, the Ottomans started to lose their military superiority over the West. The Ottoman Empire failed to win two wars against the Russian and Austrian Empires which concluded with the treaties of Carlowitz (Karlofça) in 1699 and Passarowitz (Pasarofça) in 1718. These two wars alerted the Ottomans to Western military changes and the resulting shift in the balance of power between the Ottoman Empire and the West. To preserve the Ottoman geographical boundaries in the West, the Ottoman state needed political alliances and the Ottoman army needed information on Western military technology. These needs encouraged the Ottomans to increase their participation in Western diplomacy and their observation of Western military technology.

An Ottoman treatise, which was written about the time of the Passarowitz treaty and presented to the Sultan, documented the increasing Ottoman concern with Western military successes. The document contained an imaginary conversation between a Christian and an Ottoman officer who compared their military strength.[2] The officers discussed the military and political situation of the period and gave reasons for the Ottoman defeats. The Ottoman officer presented the failure of the Ottoman state to observe the prescriptions of Sharia and traditional laws as the immediate cause of Ottoman defeats. The decline in Ottoman military organization became evident as the officers compared their armies. The officers ended the conversation by stating the need for Ottoman military reform; this reform was to be guided temporarily by Christian officers to save time. As the Ottomans discussed the feasibility of such reform, the military successes of Peter the Great who had reformed the Russian army after the Western model convinced the Ottomans to follow a similar pattern.[3]

In order to observe the West and participate in Western diplomacy, the Ottomans dispatched embassies to Europe more and more frequently. The reports of these Ottoman ambassadors reveal the drastic change in Ottoman perceptions of the West; they present a unique view of Ottoman officials as they came into contact with various aspects of Western civilization.[4]

The Ottoman encounter with the rising West is set within the context of one such embassy sent to Paris in 1720–1721. The Ottoman ambassador Yirmisekiz Çelebi Mehmed Efendi was dispatched to France to notify the French that the Ottoman state had authorized them to repair the Church of the Holy Sepulcher in Jerusalem. The actual aim of the embassy, however, was different; it was "to visit fortresses and factories, and to make a thorough study of means of civilization and education, and report on those suitable for application in the Ottoman Empire."[5] This embassy account, the first document written by an Ottoman official with the aim of observing and understanding the West, was the "first window opening to the West."[6] In the account, the differences between the French and Ottoman societies emerge through their curiosity toward each other, their public-private distinctions, their use of space, their technological levels, and the gifts they give each other.

The uniqueness of this embassy to Paris in capturing the changing Ottoman orientation to the West emerges when this embassy is compared with the Ottoman embassies to the West preceding and succeeding it. Comparable Ottoman embassies to the West were the embassy of Kara Mehmed Paşa to Vienna in 1665 and the embassy of Yirmisekiz Çelebizade Said Efendi to Stockholm in 1732–1733. The embassy of Mehmed Paşa to fulfill a diplomatic obligation of the peace treaty and the embassy of Said Efendi to collect the Swedish debt to the Ottoman Empire did not have purposes that were conducive to receptivity. Mehmed Efendi, who was sent to France to observe French society, was more perceptive. The intellectual background of Mehmed Efendi also contributed to his receptivity—Mehmed Efendi, as a "man of the pen," was more observant of a foreign society than a "man of the sword" like Mehmed Paşa. The nature of these foreign societies affected Ottoman receptivity as well; France, as a potential ally of the Ottoman Empire and as the cultural center of the West, had more to offer the Ottomans than Austria and Sweden. Since Austria was a former Ottoman enemy, the Ottoman ambassador limited his observations to assessing Austrian military strength. Sweden was a potential ally to the Ottoman Empire; the Ottoman ambassador did not have to be constrained in his observations and could therefore report on Swedish society at large. Yet, unlike France, there were not many observable cultural events and technological developments in Sweden at the time.

Two patterns emerge in the Ottoman response to the West during the eighteenth century. As a consequence of their increasing observation of the West, the Ottomans reproduced Western palace designs and the printing press, yet failed to duplicate other imported Western technological products such as textiles and watches. Several factors contribute to this result. The Ottomans had, in fact, tried to start clock and textile production to rival and curb the expansion of Western commerce in the eighteenth century. But cheap mass-produced Western clocks and watches available in Ottoman markets inhibited domestic production—Western competition pushed out the local product. Ottoman textile production met a similar fate; the West also carefully guarded technological information from the Ottomans. The printing press did not have the same fate for a number of reasons. The Ottoman state drew on the experiences of the Ottoman minorities, who had already established their own printing presses in the Ottoman Empire, to found the first Ottoman printing press. The market for books was also much smaller than that for textiles; the Ottoman press expanded the market for books rather than competing with the West for the existing market.

Western influence starts to spread into Ottoman society in the eighteenth century after it is observed, approved, and adopted by Ottoman dignitaries. Foreign residents and Ottoman minorities, who had always communicated with the West, could not produce the same effect. Social influence results from communication: foreign residents in Constantinople, who had the most knowledge of the West, faced the greatest number of obstacles in communicating their knowledge to Ottoman society. As foreign representatives, they lived in special quarters and were suspected of being spies by the Ottomans— Janissary guards assigned by the Ottoman state accompanied them wherever they went. Ottoman minorities, required to live in their own neighborhoods, could not easily communicate with the rest of Ottoman society either; their different religion reduced their credibility. Ottoman dignitaries had no such restrictions in space, religion, or language in communicating with the society at large. On the contrary, through their extensive households consisting of hundreds of people and their extensive properties throughout the Empire, the Ottoman dignitaries penetrated Ottoman society and communicated their views at all levels. When the Ottoman dignitaries started changing their perceptions of the West, the perception of Ottoman society changed with them.

1

Initiation of the Embassy and the Voyage

The Christian states have always been in communication, sending each other ambassadors. In this manner, they are kept well-informed on each other's intended course of actions and true state of affairs. In particular, all Christian nations have sent ambassadors to the Exalted [Ottoman] state to draw and communicate information. As the advantage [to these states] of sending ambassadors was certain and incontestable as stated above, and as the Ottoman state could not neglect this advantage, the noble Grand Vezir reflected upon this (advantage) and decided to send an ambassador to the lands of the French.[1]

At the beginning of the eighteenth century, the Ottomans had just been defeated in a war against Austria, Poland, Venice, and Russia which concluded with the treaty of Carlowitz in 1699.[2] The Ottomans could not win the war against Venice and Austria which resulted in the Passarowitz treaty.[3] These conflicts revealed Russia and Austria as formidable threats to the Ottoman Empire. The Ottomans therefore tried to form alliances against the Russians and Austrians.[4]

France was the most plausible state for the Ottomans to form an alliance with. Among the Western powers on the continent, France was the only significant power with the same adversaries as the Ottoman Empire: Russia and Austria. France had also maintained long, satisfactory diplomatic relations with the Ottoman Empire. French trade relations in the Ottoman territories were also successful.[5] If an alliance were formed with France against the Austrians, Austria would be restrained from waging war against the Ottoman Empire, fearing retaliation from France. This evaluation of the international context was the main reason for the Ottomans to initiate an embassy to France. This scheme was not actually feasible for France, however. The traditional policy of France had been to encourage the Ottoman Empire to get involved with the adversaries of France, act in concert with the Ottomans when French interests required it, yet never enter into a formal alliance with the Ottoman Empire.[6]

Ottomans needed to participate in European diplomacy to form alliances with Western powers. The need for this participation increased in the eighteenth century as the Ottomans started to face defeats in the West. During the reign of Ahmed III (1703–1730), the Ottoman Grand Vezir Nevşehirli Damad İbrahim Paşa tried to maintain peace in order to train the Ottoman Empire in the military arts of the West. He also tried to explore the value of Western connections.[7] He stated that Austria and Russia had to be restrained and this could be done through joining forces with France. Camilly[8] quotes İbrahim Paşa as saying

> the two empires [French and Ottoman] united [could] determine the order of the universe; that nothing has the power to undermine them as long as the fine understanding between them subsist; that the power of the German Empire is not composed of anything more than combined pieces which could easily be disunited; that it was not long ago when he [the German Emperor] was not considered in Europe more than just the mayor of Vienna . . . , that he had just recently been given a part of Sicily where he boasted to have a navy, but that the united forces of France and that of His Highness would keep this power in its place and destroy it before it could fly on its wings.

İbrahim Paşa openly wanted to join forces with France. He gave the French the authorization to repair the Latin Church of the Holy Sepulcher in order to create the pretext for sending an embassy and establishing new diplomatic ties with France. The pretext itself was important as well; Louis XIV had waited twenty-eight years for this authorization and had not been able to get it.[9]

İbrahim Paşa formulated the internal and external policies of the empire for thirteen years, as Sultan Ahmed III kept aloof from conducting state affairs. His era was one of peace and stability and was named the Tulip Era by the Turkish historian Ahmed Refik[10] because of the great interest in raising tulips during this period. The predominant interest beside tulips was the maintenance of internal and external peace. Treatises in history and literature, translations of Eastern and Western works also flourished as Ottomans enjoyed peace and sought the reasons behind the recent Ottoman defeats. As the rapid turnover within the chain of high Ottoman administrative command[11] declined, the internal stability of the Ottoman Empire increased. İbrahim Paşa maintained his firm control over the Ottoman administration by appointing a number of his relatives to important administrative posts[12]—one of his son-in-laws was the grant admiral while another was the secretary of internal affairs.[13]

In external affairs, İbrahim Paşa observed the West more closely than his predecessors, and met frequently with the English, Dutch, and French ambassadors in Constantinople. He initiated additional receptions and festivities in honor of the Western ambassadors besides the standard royal reception. Otto-man ambassadors were dispatched to Vienna and Paris to follow and report on developments in the West. This increased interest in the West was reflected in the Ottoman terminology used to address Western rulers: beside the usual clichés[14] the decrees of the Sultan now contained additional phrases[15] like "our grand, dignified friend" or "our great friend." In all, the era of İbrahim Paşa's vezirate (1718–1730) marked the first change in Ottoman attitudes toward the West from haughtiness to reconciliation, from indifference to attention, and from that of a ruler to that of a participant. This era is consid-ered the first stage of modernization in Turkey by many historians.[16]

The status of the Ottoman diplomatic representatives sent to the West also increased in the eighteenth century. Before then, Ottoman dispatches were "envoys" recruited from heralds, men trained in the Palace, or cham-berlains.[17] These envoys held symbolic functions such as sending or receiving letters, confirming treaties, or attending coronations. The six previous Otto-man dispatches to France were such envoys. These envoys were sent by Süleyman to François I in 1533, Selim II to Charles IX in 1571, Murad III to Henri III in 1581, Mehmed III to Henri IV in 1601 and to Louis XIII in 1607, and finally Mehmed IV to Louis XIV in 1669.[18] Of these, the last Ottoman envoy had roused great curiosity in France: Müteferrika Süleyman Ağa invoked a new fashion "à la turque" at the court of Louis XIV.[19]

In the eighteenth century, the Ottoman representatives were given more responsibilities; they had to conduct diplomacy, observe the foreign country, and determine possible courses of action for the Ottoman Empire. These representatives were now given the title of military judges and referred to as "ambassadors." The highest chain of Ottoman command, consisting of the Sultan, Grand Vezir, secretary in charge of foreign affairs, and head trans-lator,[20] selected the ambassador to be sent to the West. The ambassadors were recruited, according to the requirements of the situation, from among Otto-man officials in high administrative positions. The position and the person holding it had to be high enough to be known by the Ottoman chain of command who made the choice. The ambassadors were often chosen from among those who "were in the service of the Ottoman state and had attained knowledge of the arrangements of discourse and the intrigues of Christians."[21]

The need to send an Ottoman ambassador to France emerged for a variety of reasons. Primarily, the Ottomans wanted to place a check on Austria by signing an alliance with France. The Knights of Malta were also constantly pillaging Muslim vessels; the Ottomans wanted France to put pressure on the Knights to stop their pillaging.[22] Technologically, the Ottomans wanted to observe French civilization to account for their military success. Since the French had not encountered the Ottomans in any recent conflict, the Ottoman pride was not challenged to react against and resist observing French society. These reasons could not be and were not made public because of the reactions they would have drawn from Ottomans and other states. The ostensible reasons for the embassy to France were therefore to convey the authorization for the reparation of the Church of the Holy Sepulcher by the French and to negotiate for the release of Ottoman slaves held in French vessels.

The Marquis de Bonnac, French ambassador to the Porte, had been notified of the authorization during an audience with İbrahim Paşa.[23] He was also told that the Sultan had manifested the desire to send an ambassador to the French king for the notification of this authorization. Bonnac stated "that the departure of the ambassador should be postponed until the completion of the repair of the church, and that he did not have any imperial order on the subject— although he did not doubt the ambassador would be impressively received after the brilliant signs of friendship which had been given to the King by the Sultan."[24] Since the Ottomans had been thinking of sending an ambassador for some time, and had probably given the authorization merely to facilitate this assignment, they reputedly designated a head-chamberlain named Kara İnci as ambassador the day after the audience with Bonnac.[25] Bonnac, taken very much by surprise, heard that "the choice of the Porte was a man without consequence because the ambassador of the Emperor and the bailo of Venice witnessed great discontent and extreme jealousy at the sending of an important person."[26]

The French had causes for reservations as well. The timing of the embassy was bad for France. Politically, France was trying to approach Austria, not form an alliance against it. Financially, the French treasury was impoverished, and the Royal Bank had to suspend payments causing public unrest. Moreover, the plague was killing thousands, and the French had had a bad harvest season. Because of these factors, the French foreign minister Dubois sent a letter on the fourth of November, 1720, advising Bonnac to dissuade the Ottomans from sending an ambassador by invoking the plague. His letter reached Constantinople after the Ottoman ambassador had left.[27] Meanwhile, Bonnac, while awaiting orders from France, told İbrahim Paşa that if the Porte chose a person of mediocre importance to send, Bonnac would not assist him on his voyage, but if a person of distinction were sent, he would do all he could to facilitate the voyage. The Porte reconsidered its choice and officially nominated another Ottoman, Yirmisekiz Çelebi Mehmed Efendi as the Ottoman ambassador to the court of the child King Louis XV.

The French were satisfied with this choice. The Marquis de Bonnac described Mehmed Efendi in a letter to the French foreign ministry.

MEHEMET EFFENDY
TEFTERDAR.
Ambassadeur Extraordinaire de la Porte,
vers le Roy très Chrétien Louis XV. en 1721.

P. Boitard del. *et Sculp.*

Paris chez O. Heuvre M.d d'estamp. rue d'anjou la derniere P. Cochere a gauche entrant par cells Dauph.
C.P.R.

Engraving of Yirmisekiz Çelebi Mehmed Efendi. The engraving was made during Mehmed Efendi's stay in Paris. (*Phot. Bibl. Nat., Paris*)

11

He appears to me a man of wit, versed in the affairs of the empire and having knowledge about strangers. He is a man of fifty years, with agreeable visage, long black beard that has started to whiten; he is very polite, a quality not easily found here. I once gave him a meal and he wanted to give me one and gave one which was magnificent.[28]

Yirmisekiz Çelebi Mehmed Efendi[29] was the son of the Georgian Süleyman Ağa, the head-keeper of the Sultan's mastiffs, an important post within the Ottoman administration because of its proximity to the Sultan. His father was an Ottoman, not a subject, a distinction based on occupation and consequent taxation. Those employed by the state were not taxed and had the distinguished social status of being Ottomans. They usually had a disciplined education and Ottoman administrative experience, and their power and status varied in relation to their proximity to the Sultan. Mehmed Efendi, being the son of such an Ottoman, was born in Adrianople. He joined the Janissary corps and was known as Yirmisekiz because he belonged to the twenty-eighth battalion of the Janissaries. He was promoted to the ranks of colonel and chief officer of the court of justice. Since he was literate and learned, he acquired the rank of Muslim teacher. He was then appointed the superintendent of the cannon foundry. Yirmisekiz also wrote poems under the pseudonym Feyzi. In 1718, he was present at the signing of the Passarowitz treaty as the second plenipotentiary.

Mehmed Efendi was appointed the first Ottoman ambassador to Paris on the nineteenth of August, 1719.[30] His most important qualifications were his being an Ottoman with a specific background as a Janissary, a literate and learned man having financial experience, and one who had been to the West before as an Ottoman diplomat. As a Janissary, he was qualified as a high-ranking military officer; as a literate and learned man, he had knowledge in the religious sciences and was able to comprehend the physical sciences. His inclination for poetry signaled his good command of the language. Finally, his presence during the peace negotiations in Austria qualified him as an Ottoman with the rare experience of having been to the West on a diplomatic mission.

Socially, other aspects of his specific background must have influenced the chain of command to choose him from among other well-qualified candidates. He had worked together with the Grand Vezir during the Passarowitz treaty negotiations. The Grand Admiral was also his close friend. Upon Mehmed Efendi's return from Paris, the Admiral personally came to the galley to welcome him.[31] Mehmed Efendi stopped at Chios on his return from Paris because the governor was also a close friend of his.[32] Hence, Mehmed

Efendi had important friends and connections within the Ottoman administration which must have facilitated his selection as the Ottoman ambassador to France.

Ottoman officials spent a long time getting prepared for their embassies. The personal preparation of the Ottoman official involved taking care of his familial, economic, and social affairs. The official preparation included consulting with the Ottoman administration, and organizing his retinue and provisions for the embassy. Although there is no information on Mehmed Efendi's personal preparation for the embassy, except his decision to take his son with him, his embassy account suggests he might have consulted some Ottoman books on the West. Mehmed Efendi most probably also read the manuscript prepared by an Ottoman official who had been with the Ottoman embassy to Vienna after the treaty of Passarowitz.

During their travel to Paris, Mehmed Efendi and his retinue stopped in Charenton. In his embassy account, Mehmed Efendi stated[33] that "the *Atlas Minor* (of Mercatur and Hondius) which has been translated into Turkish by the late Katip Çelebi contains a strange anecdote on Charenton. There reputedly is a location in town where, if someone shouts, he could hear his voice echoed thirteen times." When he inquired about this strange event, the townspeople said they had never heard such a thing in their lives. Wondering if the location had disappeared with time, Mehmed Efendi was puzzled about the inclusion of this anecdote in the *Atlas Minor*. Yet this puzzlement benefits his reader who acquires information on Mehmed Efendi's background and probable preparation for the embassy.

One contemporary Ottoman account of the West Mehmed Efendi could also have read is one by an unknown official of the Ottoman embassy to Vienna after the treaty of Passarowitz.[34] Mehmed Efendi had participated in the negotiations of this treaty which stipulated an embassy exchange between the Austrian and the Ottoman Empires. In the account, Austrian military fortifications on the route are described in great detail—probably for Ottoman military intelligence purposes. The descriptions strike a sad note when the narrator observes a minaret converted into a clock tower by the Austrians. Since Mehmed Efendi was not going into former enemy territory or former Ottoman territory, he was spared such observations. Two descriptions in this Austrian embassy account deviate from the militaristic tone. In one, the narrator notes, with great astonishment, the "forked girl" he saw who had two heads and four arms[35]—better known today as Siamese twins. In the other description, the burial ceremony of the king's mother is explained with great interest.[36] "They (the Austrians) let her body sit for three days, took out her intestines, and filled the body with herbs before the burial," the account states. "Everyone is required to dress in black for an entire year after the death." These two sources might have provided Mehmed Efendi with additional insight into the societies of the West.

The Ottoman state clearly defined the official preparation for the embassy by protocol. The preparation started with the formal appointment of the Ottoman official by the chain of command to represent the Ottoman Empire. The official then consulted the files kept by the Ottoman administration on previous envoys sent abroad. These files gave information about "what funds, supplies, and provisions had been granted in the past, and what precedents had been established."[37] According to these files, the official was given funds and provisions depending on the size of his retinue and the length and nature of his embassy. Valuable goods were lent to the official and his retinue for the duration of the voyage.[38] These goods, mostly inlaid in gold and silver with precious metals, symbolized Ottoman wealth and power. The size of the retinue was another symbol of grandeur; it increased with the status of the official. The retinue constituted a self-sufficient unit with separate groups taking care of provision and preparation of food, upkeep of the possessions, supervision of health, maintenance of security, provision of translation, and financial administration of the retinue. Mehmed Efendi's retinue consisted of approximately one hundred persons.[39]

After the provisions, funds, supplies, and the retinue were organized, the official had an audience with the Sultan. He was accompanied into the Sultan's presence by the Grand Vezir and the Grand Müftü of the capital. During the audience, the Sultan's authority was bestowed symbolically on the official as he was dressed in a robe of honor. The official also received the Sultan's letter to the ruler of the host state. The embassy was centered around this letter which was the most important public document. Subsequent protocol in the visited country depended on the importance attributed to the sender of the letter.[40] The official also received the private oral orders of the Sultan during this audience. These orders must have pertained to the hidden reasons of the embassy. After this procedure was completed, the official and his retinue left Constantinople with a parade.

The accounts of these embassies provided Ottoman history with some of its finest documents, namely *sefaretname*s. These are the public reports prepared and presented by ambassadors or officials in their retinue who were sent to foreign states as representatives of the Ottoman state. These reports usually detail the whole journey from the departure from Constantinople to the observations on the country visited, with frequent descriptions of the statesmen met, places visited, and events and deeds that occurred. The *sefaretname* was primarily written for the Sultan, the Ottoman chain of command, top

Ottoman administrators concerned with foreign relations. The nature of the audience determined the tone of the report; all reports were reserved and formal.

The embassy accounts were an important source of information on foreign societies for the Ottomans. These embassy accounts were not the only source of information the Ottomans had of foreign societies, however. In the East, the governors of the border provinces, in the North, the Crimean Khans, and in the West, the voivodes of Walachia and Moldavia, the Ragusan republic, and the Transylvanian kingdom that had recognized Ottoman sovereignty were responsible for providing information about the bordering states. This information was specific in nature: it focused on the military power, the internal conflicts, and the foreign relations of the bordering states. Ottoman merchants who were in Europe for trade purposes also reported the events they saw and the news they heard to the Porte. Their information evolved from the economic sphere and was limited to their individual experiences and interpretations. The Porte gathered information on the political conditions of the European states through Ottoman dragomans assigned to the European embassies in Constantinople.[41] The dragomans could only transmit the information European ambassadors wished to convey.

Another possible source of information on foreign cultures is the accounts of Ottoman travelers and Ottoman captives in Europe. Such accounts occur very rarely in Ottoman history: one such account is provided by a well-known Ottoman traveler Evliya Çelebi.[42] Having traveled in Europe during the second half of the seventeenth century, Evliya Çelebi provides ample information on the towns he traveled to and on the events he encountered. These accounts, however, were usually written after the actual completion of the travels, with the purpose of entertaining a general audience. The value of the information they contain is therefore difficult to assess.

Other Ottoman sources of information are difficult to document. The Ottoman official correspondence avoided mentioning the source of information; other information was conveyed orally. In most official Ottoman correspondence, such as a letter between the Sultan and the Grand Vezir,[43] information on the West was discussed without referring to the source. The documents started by stating that the information "had been known to them"[44] without stating how they came to know it. The Ottoman espionage system could have been one such possible source of information. The existence of Ottoman spies can be documented through Ottoman registers. Some finance registers of the Palace[45] contain records of names of "spies," sometimes with the person or institution to whom they are attached. In one specific register, there are eleven entries where each spy listed received one thousand *akças* and an embroidered

Brusan garment. This documents that spies were used to gather information, but there is no information on how and where they were employed.

It is very difficult to trace orally communicated information. However, the correspondence between European ambassadors in Constantinople and their governments contains frequent references to their communication with the Porte. These references sometimes provide the specific oral communication the ambassadors had with the Sultan. For example, during his audience with the Grand Vezir, the French ambassador Bonnac found out that Mehmed Efendi had told the vezir about some aspects of the military maneuver he had witnessed which did not appear in his embassy account.[46]

Ottoman embassy accounts are the only systematic reporting of direct Ottoman experiences of the West. The major limitation of embassy accounts as an information source derive from their official status. The ambassadors were official representatives of the Ottoman state when they composed these accounts and they were written for an audience of Ottoman dignitaries. The information revealed in the accounts is therefore very formal, well-structured, and very carefully written. They contain only neutral descriptive information on formal events with very few evaluative remarks.

This formality of embassy accounts is a feature of all official Ottoman correspondence. The imperial orders of Sultans to other rulers or to their commanders are just as formal. The limitations of formal accounts as information sources become evident when compared to informal correspondence. There is sufficient documentation on the informal correspondence of the Ottoman Sultans. The correspondence provides valuable information on perceptions, evaluations, and criticisms of the Sultan. Such information is never revealed in formal accounts. The informal correspondence of Sultan Ahmed III illustrates this point.

Sultan Ahmed III corresponded very frequently with his Grand Vezir İbrahim Paşa on a variety of subjects. In one letter,[47] he stated

> I talked to the paşa [asking him for the acquisition of some money], his behavior is like that of a swashbuckler, he has not been [properly] bred in state conduct. He restricts himself [when communicating with me], yet how he treats the officals [I send him] I do not know. I hope you come as soon as possible and put things in order. He gave me one equipped horse and one bare one; the equipment on the horse was of the lowest quality. [My *sultan* daughter] did not give me even a single clog. . . . My son Süleyman was not even given a pony; not that we would have accepted more gifts than that [had they given a pony]. What would they lose if they gave [even so little]; is it intentional or out of their extreme indigence I am utterly amazed. . . . I resent having ever visited [my *sultan* daughter].

The Sultan's criticisms were very personal and reflected the frustrations he had with people surrounding him. In correspondence with his Grand Vezir, Sultan Ahmed III bitterly complained about the formality of the Palace during an illness.[48]

> I go out to one of the chambers. Forty chamber members line up. I have my trousers on. It is never comfortable. My sword-bearer needs to throw them out [of the chamber] leaving only three or four men [or] I should sit in the small chamber.

These two informal accounts reveal personal criticisms and judgments—a dimension lacking in embassy accounts.

Embassy accounts provide information on only a specific part of the interaction with a foreign society. This specific part is determined by the particular motives behind the embassies; the embassy of Mehmed Efendi was to observe French civilization. Mehmed Efendi, as an Ottoman ambassador, could only provide a formal, diplomatic account of his embassy. As a learned Ottoman, he exercised the Ottoman concept of politeness and rationed his words with utmost terseness. The embassy accounts should be analyzed with caution as very valuable, albeit formal sources of information on Ottoman perceptions of the West.

Because of his exclusive Ottoman audience, Mehmed Efendi was duly formal and reserved in his report. The Marquis de Bonnac wanted to translate and publish the report in France; the addition of a French audience to the exclusive Ottoman audience made Mehmed Efendi doubly careful. This was a new practice, as previous host states were not given copies of Ottoman embassy accounts. The first known embassy account is that of Kara Mehmed Paşa who was sent to Vienna in 1665.

The original report of Mehmed Efendi to the Sultan and the Grand Vezir has not yet been discovered. The earliest manuscript, dating from 1722–1723, contains three empty sections with a heading stating a picture is to follow; the actual report must have been illustrated.[49] There are twelve additional manuscripts and seven printed accounts of Mehmed Efendi's account.[50]

Among the existing editions of Mehmed Efendi's embassy account, this study uses the two Ottoman texts printed in 1841 and 1866 along with the recently edited French text. The Ottoman text printed in Constantinople is the 1866 version titled *Sefaretname-i Fransa;* it was transcribed by Abdullah Uçman in 1975. The other Ottoman text printed in Paris is the 1841 version titled *Relation de l'ambassade de Mehemet Effendi en France* in French, and *Mehmed Efendi'nin Sefaretnamesi* in Ottoman. It was published in 1841 for the Ecole Royale et Speciale des Langues Orientales Vivantes. The French text was edited by Gilles Veinstein in 1981 and titled *Le Paradis des Infideles*. Veinstein bases his work primarily on the text that had been translated by Galland and sent to the Royal Library by Bonnac.[51] He also incorporated two other versions: the manuscript sent by Bonnac to Comte de Morville, the state secretary of foreign relations,[52] and the final unedited text in the French archives.[53]

One additional manuscript in a private library needs to be mentioned. Parts of it have been edited and published in an abridged form.[54] The editor states that this manuscript was dictated and hand-corrected by Mehmed Efendi himself. The only page published from this manuscript to verify this statement does indeed contain a correction on the margin. The editor also notes that the language of this manuscript is less elaborate than the printed editions where most Turkish words are replaced by their Persian or Arabic equivalents. It is unfortunately impossible to assess the nature, scope, and significance of these corrections, or the possible variations in the account itself without studying the manuscript. The abridged text does not provide the manuscript in its original form.

The *sefaretname* started with a prayer to God asking his protection for the duration of the voyage, and ended with prayer thanking God for that protection. This seemed to be a standard Islamic procedure.[55] Mehmed Efendi wrote the report in the first-person plural, except when he quoted what he had said. This encompassed his retinue and himself. This form also reflected the Ottoman conception of politeness and dignity. When Mehmed Efendi referred to himself, he used the phrase "this humble servant."[56] Mehmed Efendi's language was also economical. In keeping with the precision of his descriptions, he avoided value-laden words when interpreting a situation: detained for almost two months by the quarantine, he just remarked that he had to "put on the robe of patience"[57] or when traveling by land under bad weather conditions, he stated that if he had to recite all the hardships he had to go through, "nine sheets as large as the nine skies would not have been enough to write on."[58]

Mehmed Efendi's use of Persian increased especially when he described his emotional state: he scattered Persian verses relevant to the situation.[59] Meanwhile, his only reference to religion was his recital of a *hadis* which, though attributed to the Prophet, appeared in medieval times. Mehmed Efendi's citation was significant in relation to his period. He recited the *hadis* "this world is the prison of the believer and the paradise of the unbeliever" when he was very impressed with the park of Marly.[60]

Mehmed Efendi's journey consisted of three stages: the voyage to Paris, the stay in Paris and its environs, and the voyage from Paris.

When describing the route[61] of the voyage, Mehmed Efendi's account

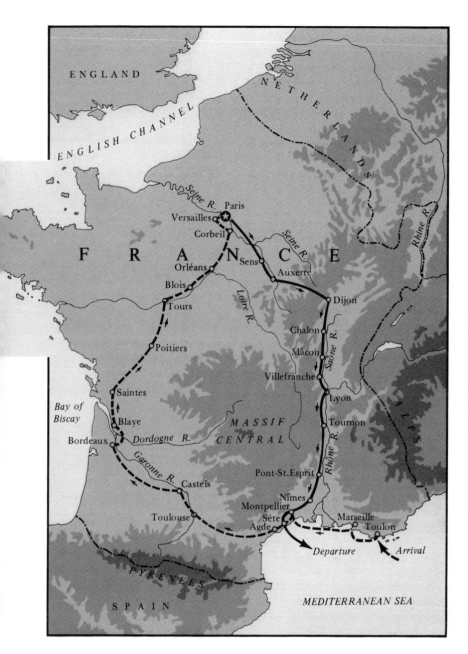

Mehmed Efendi's route to and from Paris. The dotted line indicates his route to Paris, the solid line his return route. (*Map drawn by H. Desmet-Grégoire,* Le Divan Magique, *Paris 1980.*)

stated the precise names and special characteristics of the places along the way. Either he or someone in his retinue must have kept a diary at least to note the French names that were not at all correlated to the Ottoman language. These names were usually spelled out phonetically. The route of Mehmed Efendi and his large retinue combined sea and land travel; they traveled from Constantinople to Montpellier by sea, and after the quarantine they took the Languedoc canal (Canal de Provence) to Bordeaux, and continued overland to Paris. On their return, they traveled by land to Lyon, by the Rhone river to St. Esprit, and then by land to Montpellier where they embarked a vessel to Constantinople. Their travels over water obviated the problems they would have faced by traveling during fall and winter.[62] Navigation was easier with favorable winds in the fall whereas one had to face difficult road conditions— as Mehmed Efendi journeyed from Bordeaux to Paris by land, he stated that "there was not a single thing left among our attendants and goods that was not soaked and soiled with mud."[63] He probably would have faced more difficulties and would have consequently formed more unfavorable impressions had he traveled entirely overland. The difficulties involved in such travel were stated by another Ottoman ambassador Ahmed Azmi Efendi in his *sefaret-name* to Prussia.[64] In addition to a short quarantine, the Ottoman embassy had to pass through Austria where officials tried to tax them and villagers tried to charge them for things Ottomans considered free accommodation for ambassadors. The Ottoman state regarded foreign ambassadors in the Ottoman Empire as guests; these ambassadors were provided with free food and travel accommodations and were even given a daily allowance. Ottoman ambassadors were therefore disappointed when the Western states did not reciprocate the hospitality of the Ottoman state. It was very unpleasant for these ambassadors to find themselves often in financial difficulty as they were expected to pay for everything. Ahmed Azmi and his retinue often had to change route or speed up just to avoid these charges.

Sea travel provided different experiences for Ottoman ambassadors. On his voyage from Toulon to Paris, Mehmed Efendi's first encounters in France focused on three events: the quarantine he was subjected to, the Languedoc canal he traveled through, and the tide he observed for the first time. The first French imposition on the Ottomans was the quarantine. When the Ottoman embassy arrived in France, the French abstained from even approaching the Ottomans and this reception must have been disconcerting. The quarantine required a waiting period of forty days for all visitors from the East regardless of religion, nationality, or status. It became institutionalized as the disparity in the conceptions of public health and hygiene between the West and the East grew.[65] The Europeans rigorously applied the quarantine to control the possibility and impact of the plague, while the Ottomans passively accepted the plague as the unchangeable will of God. D'Ohsson[66] observed this attitude with astonishment, stating that in the Ottoman Empire, "occurences in nature (like the plague) provide a new degree of confidence in the dogma of fatalism. The parents do not ever abandon the sick bed. This provides an example of perfect resignation to the decrees of the heavens." The quarantine was conceptually irrelevant in the Ottoman world-view.

When Mehmed Efendi and his retinue arrived at Toulon, they were informed by the French about the plague in the Provence region. The French, after an initial quarantine in Toulon, proposed changing the route to Paris because of the plague. They proposed a voyage through the Languedoc canal.[67] Mehmed Efendi accepted this proposal, not on the grounds of the danger presented by the plague, but because he did not want to cause any embarrassment to the French. The French reaction to the plague and their great concern amazed Mehmed Efendi. He described the quarantine in great detail:[68]

> When there is an epidemic in the lands of these people, they do not mix with the persons coming from other lands for a long time. They converse with these persons without touching them. . . . They do not approach these persons before the lapse of twenty, thirty, and sometimes forty days because of their extreme fear of contracting the disease. They call this separation time quarantine at Nazarto (lazaret).

Mehmed Efendi must have assumed that his stay in Toulon for over a week to be the actual quarantine. He was very surprised when, sailing to Sète to resume his journey, he found himself confined to the island of Maguelonne in an old cathedral for another forty days.[69] Yet his only formal comment on the situation was the statement that he decided to suffer the inconvenience with calm since there was nothing he could do about it.

Although Mehmed Efendi did not detail his reactions to the quarantine, contemporary French accounts contain his actions. Mehmed Efendi was very upset about the length of the quarantine. He asked for a reduction stating that "he would not have thought to be sent on exile when he was named ambassador before a great prince like the French Emperor."[70] The French, however, were very adamant since the plague had been imported on a ship coming from the East,[71] and because they applied the quarantine to everyone without exception. Mehmed Efendi put up with the length of the quarantine, claimed Lenoir,[72] his translator, "after having seen the Dutch gazettes which reported the fear of the inhabitants upon the arrival of the Ottoman ministry in Paris who not only came from a country where the plague reigned every day, but who also were going to pass through the kingdom." There was no explanation about how Mehmed Efendi had access to the gazette except Lenoir's statement that he wanted to see all the European journals from the moment of his arrival in France. Since chronicles, journals, and periodicals were not published by the Ottomans at the time,[73] his interest in and knowledge of European gazettes could be a consequence, in theory, of his privileged position within the Ottoman administration. He might have had access to information about Europe through his position. On his trip to Austria two years earlier, he might have perceived the importance of such publications. Mehmed Efendi's access to Dutch gazettes, however, was a puzzle even to Lenoir. This puzzle might be solved by studying the travel companions of Mehmed Efendi. In Toulon, some people asked Mehmed Efendi for permission to join his retinue for the journey to Paris.[74] These people, who had been stranded in Toulon for months due to the plague, consisted of the consul of France to Tripoli with his wife and servant, six French consuls or vice-consuls, five British, and one Dutch.[75] Probably the Dutchman provided him with the information. This event was the first indication of Mehmed Efendi's interest in the French. His exclusion of this event from his account, on the other hand, may have been due to the public nature of the *sefaretname,* which was to be presented to the Ottoman Sultan and the French ambassador.

After the forty-day quarantine on the island, Mehmed Efendi continued his journey to Paris through the Languedoc canal, which marked his first encounter with French technology. The canal connected the Mediterranean Sea and the Atlantic Ocean through an artificial river basin and various elevated pools. Mehmed Efendi, very impressed, defined the canal in his account:

> This thing called canal by the French is one river created by collecting others from the sides and the environs. . . . The canal makes reaching the sea of the Ocean from the Mediterranean through cities and land possible without setting foot on land.[76]

Rather than letting this information suffice, Mehmed Efendi continued to give a very detailed explanation of how the canal actually operated and solved the natural obstacles of height differences and mountains on its path. He must have asked for and gathered a substantial amount of information on the canal. The length of the account foreshadows Mehmed Efendi's interest and accuracy in describing the state of other examples of French technology.

The last encounter he noted reflected the difference between the French and Ottoman physical environments. The tide of the Atlantic Ocean is very conspicuous during the day. The changes of sea level on the Mediterranean during the day are incremental, unlike the drastic changes on the Atlantic. Mehmed Efendi was therefore astonished to observe the impact of this natural phenomenon.

At this location, it was possible to view the ebb and flow [of the Ocean] which we had heard about. . . . The vessels near the shore stay on land during the ebb and float during the flow. The arriving and departing vessels note the ebb and flow times and move with the current. This is something so strange that it must be seen to be believed.[77]

2

The Cultural Interaction

On a fait aussi avec ces arbres des chambres qui ont leurs portes et leurs galeries et qui sont couvertes de verdure; enfin, on leur a donne cent sortes de figures et ils sont disposés dans une certaine ordonnance et d'une certaine manière que leur vue porte l'allégresse dans le coeur. En voyant ce jardin, je compris ce beau passage de l'Alcoran qui dit que "le monde est la prison des fidèles et le paradis des infidèles."[1]

These people are not so unpolish'd as we represent them. Tis true their Magnificence is of a different taste from ours, and perhaps of a better. I am allmost of opinion they have a right notion of Life; they consume it in Music, Gardens, Wine, and delicate eating, while we are formenting our brains with some Scheme of Politics or studying some Science to which we can never attain, or if we do, cannot persuade people to set that value upon it we do ourselves.[2]

The economic, political, and social changes in the West up to the eighteenth century changed the image of the West. The image of the West was created by the ruler and the nobility of the centralized state residing in the capital. The society and the capital redefined their lives after this image. The competition for royal attention among the nobility in eighteenth-century France fostered new forms of entertainment. Theaters emerged in special halls where the audience sat according to rank and ability to pay. Museums evolved from the collections of curiosities by the nobility. Parks and gardens developed around the city as the need for public space increased with increasing entertainment.

Private space also underwent change. The economic developments and the increased importance of the workplace led to a physical separation of the working quarters from the living quarters. Once work was out of the house, home life became privatized: space was specialized room by room as bedrooms, dining rooms, and reception rooms were formed along a corridor. The corridor was also a new invention. As rooms were specialized, the furniture in the rooms proliferated. The recent improvements in heating techniques[3] and in economic conditions altered spatial use as ceilings were raised and changed from wooden into light-colored plaster, as paneled walls gave way to papered walls, and as parquet was used on the floors. As doors became wider and leaded glass windows and mirrors became larger with better production techniques, more daylight entered the rooms. There was a total change in scale of life as everything expanded. A new sense of spaciousness developed in the West.[4]

France was the leader of this transformation. All the European states looked to France, to its art, architecture, and entertainment with wonder as did Mehmed Efendi. The French evolved a distinctive style of life, and a distinct fashion that established their sovereignty in Europe during the eighteenth century. The Marly palace and gardens, which had impressed Mehmed Efendi so much that he declared "the world is the paradise of the infidels,"[5] was considered the eighth wonder of the world throughout Europe as well. The amount of change that occurred in France during the eighteenth century was so vast that Duclos, about 1765, stated that the people who died in the beginning of the eighteenth century, if they were to come back, would not recognize Paris as far as its tables, customs, and costumes were concerned.[6] Mehmed Efendi was observing France against this background of momentous change.

Striking differences between the two societies emerged through Mehmed Efendi's observations. The French and the Ottomans had different boundaries between public and private spheres of life. In the area of entertainment, different sets of leisure activities and different conceptions of time existed. The French attended operas and ballets while the Ottomans had no such entertainments. Their music was based on a different scale. French women participated in public social life while Ottoman women did not. Temporally, the French entertainment lasted longer and was concentrated in the evenings. Art and architecture contained different uses of space and different aesthetic sensibilities. The French organized private construction geometrically and symmetrically while the Ottomans did not. The use of internal space was also different. Mehmed Efendi's perceptions of science and technology revealed the differences in the levels of scientific development. As Mehmed Efendi visited the observatory, mirror factories, the royal printing press, and the hospital for the veterans, he was encountering institutions that did not exist in the Ottoman Empire at the time. The gift exchange between the Ottomans and the French epitomized the different value orientations of the two societies; the Ottomans gave military gifts while the French reciprocated with technological products.

Mehmed Efendi's observations revealed the differences between the

Ottoman and French societies to a limited extent, however. An observation could be evaluated as ranging from pleased and surprised to knowledgeable to offended and disgusted. Mehmed Efendi only used the positive half of this spectrum. He rarely made explicit comparisons between the Ottoman and French societies. Only three such comparisons exist in the text. All these comparisons were on neutral subjects such as the physical features of sites or cities. In one comparison, Mehmed Efendi stated that the Garonne river in Bordeaux "spreads out in front of the city like the port of Istanbul."[7] While visiting the Marly gardens in Paris, the aquaduct prompted Mehmed Efendi to a comparison with "the high aquaduct in Kırkçeşme"[8]—a neighborhood in Istanbul. The last comparison involved the population of the cities of Paris and Istanbul. Mehmed Efendi noted that "Paris is not, in reality, as populous as Istanbul although the buildings are elevated and the houses numerous."[9]

Mehmed Efendi was very careful in his comparisons not to evaluate explicitly the French and Ottoman societies. His word selection, however, revealed some of the differences. His use of words was systematic—whenever he encountered a French term, he explained the term in Ottoman and used the Ottoman equivalent. If there was no Ottoman equivalent, he used the French term. In this manner, Mehmed Efendi developed his own vocabulary.

Mehmed Efendi made frequent use of Ottoman terms to describe French ones. He switched to Ottoman terminology whenever he narrated an official correspondence with the King. Although he used the term *kral* (king) to refer to Louis XV throughout his account, Mehmed Efendi chose the term *padişah of France* when he addressed the King formally.[10] *Padişah,* an Ottoman term of Persian origin, was mostly used to refer to the Ottoman sultans and those sovereigns regarded to have equal status with the Ottoman sultans. This form of address to the French king therefore indicates the high Ottoman esteem of the French king. *Kral,* the Ottoman term of Slavic origin for king, was used by the Ottomans to refer to any Christian ruler; it did not symbolically reflect the high Ottoman esteem of the ruler the way *padişah* did. The King's orders to Mehmed Efendi became "the *ferman* of the *padişah* of France to this humble servant."[11] The events Mehmed Efendi observed during his embassy often acquired an Ottoman dimension. The French military bands which played whenever he entered a town became *mehterhane*s (Ottoman military bands).[12] When the French representative asked Mehmed Efendi if they could send his baggage by land to Paris to save time in travel, Mehmed Efendi reworded this request in his narration.[13] "The French official told us," Mehmed Efendi wrote, "you hand over (your baggage) to us and *inşallahü teala* (Allah willing) we will give it back to you intact in Paris."

French entertainments provided Mehmed Efendi with additional opportunities to use Ottoman concepts. Whenever Mehmed Efendi encountered a big crowd of French people around him, he used the expression "crowded more than a wedding."[14] Ottoman weddings must have been the most crowded occasions in Ottoman society. Mehmed Efendi also specified the different French use of space in Ottoman terms. He referred to the French theatre as *rakkashane*,[15] which meant place where one watched dances.

The dictionary Mehmed Efendi developed during this embassy included many French terms in their original form. Mehmed Efendi defined the French representatives, who were sent by the King to accompany him in France, in terms of their functions. He noted that an *intentan* (Fr. intendant) was "a person who supervised the affairs of the French navy and the French people."[16] Another person Mehmed Efendi dealt frequently with was the *entüredüktör* (Fr. introducteur). "These people (the French) have a rank peculiar to them—the possessor (of the rank) is called an *entüredüktör*," Mehmed Efendi said.[17] "This person is appointed specially for the ambassadors—to welcome them, organize their processions, and take them to the King." Mehmed Efendi added that these representatives brought *kompliment* (Fr. compliment) which were "orders to give greetings and felicitations on arrival."[18] In this particular case, the greetings were from the King. Mehmed Efendi used the term *kompliment* throughout his account in its original French form with great ease. Once, he used this term together with another French term, *çerimonya* (Fr. ceremonie).[19]

Mehmed Efendi used some French terms in his account without explaining what these words meant. Some of these words were associated with the military. The Ottomans must have encountered these terms frequently enough to incorporate them into their vocabularies. These terms were *soltat* (Fr. soldat),[20] *recment* (Fr. regiment),[21] and *tranpete* (Fr. trumpette).[22] The other two terms used in their original form without an explanation were again terms Ottomans must have come across in their association with the West, *prençe* (Fr. prince),[23] and *prençize* (Fr. princesse).[24]

Mehmed Efendi had to define two French military terms he had not encountered before. One term was *süyis* (Fr. Suisse)[25] who were "the hundred soldiers with their captains who were constantly guarding the King's palace and its gates. They were [from] people [living] between France and Austria who were hired by whoever needed them." The other term Mehmed Efendi had to define was "the esteemed regiment of the King," called *şampanya* (the Regiment of Champagne).[26] Mehmed Efendi also had to define two terms explaining aspects of the French spatial organization which differed from the Ottoman. One term that had become fashionable in eighteenth-century France was the open court. *Kur* (Fr. cour)[27] meant open space, according to Mehmed Efendi. "It is a wide, pleasant green meadow filled with tall trees. These trees have been planted with such calculation that all have the same proportion and do not differ from one another . . . the King sometimes rides about there in his carriage." The Ottoman measurement of distance was also different from the French, according to Mehmed Efendi. "These people do not pay attention to hours traveled," he stated, "they say (and measure distance by) *mil* (Fr. mile).[28] These do not match one another—in some places, a mile corresponds to an hour, in others, it is less than an hour."

The differences in the way the Ottoman and French societies were structured became evident as Mehmed Efendi started to meet French officials. He tried to understand their positions within French society by comparing them to Ottoman officials. Two elements in his descriptions support this interpretation. Mehmed Efendi constantly tried to describe a French official by the office he held and the functions he served in French society. The titles of French nobility were lost on him. Mehmed Efendi stated, for example, that he had met someone who was called *Mösyö lödük* (Monsieur le Duc).[29] It would have been impossible to identify this official in French society without knowing his full title, which was "Monsieur le Duc de Bourbon." The first names of these officials were never mentioned unlike the Ottoman system. The great variation in French titles required a lot of explanation for an Ottoman audience. Mehmed Efendi had to clarify that "the nobleman who is the King's *mirahur* (master of stables) and *kaftancı* (garment keeper) is of higher esteem than all other noblemen; his rank is higher than the nobleman who is our *mihmandar* (escort)."[30] Mehmed Efendi used the titles of Ottoman officials to understand and explain the positions of French officials throughout his embassy account. He described the beauty of the palace "belonging to the *defterdar* (treasurer) of the King of Spain."[31] In Paris, Mehmed Efendi met the Duke of Biron, the lieutenant general of the French army, whom he referred to as "the *kethüda* (deputy) of the French army."[32] Similarly, the Duke of Bourbon was described as "the *kethüda* of the King."[33]

Mehmed Efendi noticed one additional characteristic of the French officials other than the offices they held. He carefully noted their blood relation to the King. The Duke of Bourbon, "deputy to the King, is a close relation of the King."[34] The Count of Toulouse[35] "is an illegitimate son of the Great King (Louis XIV). Among the Frenchmen, he is the most respected of the late King's sons; his rank is also high and respected." Another son of the late King, "a marshal duke in Bordeaux sent his deputy and did not come to visit us himself because he was a King's son."[36]

Mehmed Efendi was interested in the political position of the legitimate son and legal heir of the late King, the child King Louis XV. "The custom of these people (the French) is such that if the King has a male child, they do not crown him until he reaches puberty. Since his sovereignty is not complete, they appoint a trustworthy person his guardian and delegate authority over the state affairs to this guardian. The paternal great uncle is the *vasi* (guardian) of this one."[37] This guardian is the Duke of Orleans. The tutor of the King was the Duke of Villeroi. Mehmed Efendi used the term *lala,* tutor-manservant assigned to the care of a child, to describe Villeroi, "a wise man who has taken over the education of the King; he stays at the palace of the King, lives there, and is not for an instance separated from the King."[38] The Ottoman political system operated in a different manner. The Sultan never delegated his sovereignty even when he was not of age; there was no regency.

There were other political practices that had no equivalent in the Ottoman system. Mehmed Efendi carefully defined and used the French original of two important French political concepts with no equivalent in Ottoman. These were the political positions of ministers and privileged towns in France.

"These people (the French) have a few vezirs who are called *ministri* (Fr. ministre)," Mehmed Efendi stated.[39] "The esteem of their rank is higher than even the marshals and dukes. Each one is charged with a stipulated matter and does not intervene in the matters of others. Each one is independent in the matter he has been appointed to." Mehmed Efendi elaborated on the different functions of these ministers.[40] There was no such specialization and independence of function within the Ottoman administrative system. The Ottoman administrators were not independent in their decision making. Mehmed Efendi therefore carefully differentiated among the ministers of war and foreign relations. "They (the French) have one more vezir called *ministri de lagir* (ministre de la guerre, minister of war, Claude Leblanc)[41] who is charged with the affairs of military campaigns; he visited us." Mehmed Efendi had frequent interaction with the French foreign minister Archbishop of Cambrai Guillaume Dubois. The position of this minister was described in detail. In one instance, Mehmed Efendi referred to Dubois as "the *ministri de ta* (Fr. ministre d'état) who is charged with foreign affairs; he also supervises the ambassadors."[42] In another instance,[43] Mehmed Efendi used the term *hariciye vekili,* minister of foreign affairs, to refer to Dubois, and stated that "he, for example, has power to take precautions for war and peace, see to the affairs of all merchants, attend to the affairs of the ambassadors from all sides (of the world), and appoint or dismiss the French ambassadors who come to the Threshold of Felicity (Constantinople)." Mehmed Efendi was interested enough to inquire and acquire a lot of information on Dubois. Dubois, "an ungrateful monk,[44] is also the bishop of the Cambrai fortress. He is called *arşevek piskopos* (Fr. archevêque); *arşevek* means independent ruler."[45] Having defined the term, Mehmed Efendi used it throughout his account.

The other political concept not present in the Ottoman political system was the concept of privileged towns. Mehmed Efendi passed through the privileged towns of Toulouse and Bordeaux on his way to Paris. His descriptions of these towns were not as detailed and clear as his previous description of the ministers. Mehmed Efendi was not fully aware of the political position of privileged towns. He only noted that the King's soldiers could not enter the towns and that there were parliaments with presidents. He provided little information on the political structure of Toulouse. "The *parlment* (Fr. parlement) of the Languedoc province is in Toulouse,"[46] Mehmed Efendi noted, "they call the head (of the parliament) *prezident* (Fr. président). The King's soldiers are forbidden to enter into the town." Mehmed Efendi's treatment of the privileged town of Bordeaux was also brief.[47] He wrote "as this town too is free—the soldiers again stayed outside . . . this town too has a parliament; members of the parliament came (to visit me) but the president did not . . . he did not come because of his pretension of holding a high rank." Mehmed Efendi did not provide more information on the privileged towns. The privileged towns of France were distinct from the free cities of the Holy Roman Empire; these towns had privileges but not the independence of free cities. Mehmed Efendi's usage of the word "free city"[48] for a privileged town might have resulted from other Ottoman interactions with Europe. The association of the Ottomans with this political concept could be through the Holy Roman Empire, which had free cities and was a neighbor of the Ottoman Empire. The Ottomans could thus have been exposed to the concept through this geographical proximity. Mehmed Efendi could therefore have used this concept of a free city to define the French privileged towns; he did not provide a new definition to take this fine political distinction into account.[49]

Mehmed Efendi's use of words reflected his perceptions of the French system indirectly. As Mehmed Efendi interacted with the French, he started to narrate events that provided more information about the differences between the Ottoman and French societies. When Mehmed Efendi approached Paris, the French preparations to receive him in Paris increased. The French experience with Muslim ambassadors had been very limited and negative. The last Muslim ambassador to Paris was received in 1706; he was the Persian ambassador Mehmed Rıza Bey sent by Şah Hüseyin. This ambassador set such sharp contrasts between the cultures and provided such a background that the French expected the worst when dealing with the Ottomans. Contemporary French accounts depicted Mehmed Rıza Bey as being "cruel, eccentric, fierce, rude, unstable in his resolutions, and never willing to listen either to good reason or to good sense."[50] The Persian ambassador helped maintain the negative image of the Muslims with his insolence. His frequent use of opium made him extremely temperamental. He refused to ride in the King's carriage, and showed no interest in sightseeing in Paris. The French virtually had to throw him out of his residence to make him return to Persia.[51] When the Ottoman embassy set out, the French were apprehensive because of this negative experience. Bonnac had to state "there was a great deal of difference between Mehmed Efendi and the Persian ambassador; Mehmed Efendi had a strong inclination to render himself agreeable and he (Bonnac) knew the Grand Vezir had given Mehmed Efendi such an order."[52] Still, the French prepared very carefully. French royal inventories contained details of the reception ceremonies for the French ambassador at the Ottoman court.[53] The French used these details in drawing the principal lines of Mehmed Efendi's reception. These details were then discussed with Mehmed Efendi at length while he was resting at Charenton before his official entrance to Paris.[54]

The Ottoman and the French held different reception ceremonies. The reception and the audience with the King consisted of entering the palace, presenting the letters, exchanging compliments, and withdrawing amidst an animated palace crowd of the French nobility, men and women. In the recep-

Mehmed Efendi's entrance to Paris. The painting by Martin depicts the Ottoman ambassador and his son Said Efendi, both on horseback, at the lower left-hand side. (*Cliché: Musées de la ville de Paris* © *by SPADEM 10*)

RÉCEPTION, PAR LE SULTAN AHMED III, DE M. DE BONNAC, AMBASSADEUR DE FRANCE (13 AVRIL 1717).

Reception of the French ambassador the Marquis de Bonnac by the Ottoman Sultan Ahmed III. (*From M. C. Schefer* Mémoire Historique sur l'Ambassade de France à Constantinople par le Marquis de Bonnac, *Paris 1894; Phot. Bibl. Nat., Paris*)

tion and audience with the Ottoman Sultan, however, the Christian ambassador was served a meal in silence after entering the palace. He was honored with a sable pelisse while caftans were distributed to his retinue. Only then did he enter the reception hall to be received by the Sultan and all those around him were "immobile like statues."[55] After the exchange of words and letters, the reception was over.

These differences between the French and Ottoman receptions were evident in the engravings of the periods.[56] Ahmed III's reception of the French ambassador the Marquis de Bonnac and Louis XV's reception of the Ottoman

Reception of the Ottoman ambassador Yirmisekiz Çelebi Mehmed Efendi by the French King Louis XV, here only a child. (*Phot. Bibl. Nat., Paris*)

L'AUDIANCE DONNÉE PAR SA MAJESTÉ A MEHEMET EFFENDY AMBASSADEUR DU GRAND SULTAN ACHMET
III EMPEREURS DES TURCS AU PALAIS DES TUILLERIES LE 21 MARS 1721.

ALMANACH POUR L'ANNÉE M.DCC.XXII.

A Paris Chez F. Gerard Jollain rue St Jacques a l'Enfant Jesus

A. Le Roy sur son Throsne. B. Mr le Regent. C. Mr Le Duc de Bourbon. D. Mr Le Mal de Villeroy. E. Mr Le Pce de Conti.
F. Mr Labbé de Clermont. G. Mr Le C. Dubois. H. Mr le Comte de Toulouze. I. L'interprette. L. Son Excellence et
Sahich Mehemet son Fils. M. Les Presents.

33

ambassador Mehmed Efendi took place in diverse settings. The first notice-able difference was the size of the audiences. The Ottoman audience consisted of a small number of Ottoman officials, the members of the *divan,* officers of the chamber, and pages.[57] The French audience gathered for the reception of Mehmed Efendi, however, was much more crowded and heterogeneous. Almost all the top echelons of the nobility in Paris were present. The most important addition to the French audience were the "approximately three hundred ladies of the court placed in the grand gallery."[58] In this crowded French audience, the people did not pay total attention to the reception—many were looking at each other. This informality contrasted sharply with the gravity of the Ottoman audience. All the Ottoman officials stood motionless and fixed their gaze upon specific members of the ambassador's retinue.

The physical distance between the ambassadors and the rulers also differed. The French ambassador did not present the King's letter in person. While he stood away from the Sultan at a respectable distance by Ottoman standards, the Ottoman officials presented his letter for him. The Ottoman ambassador was able to get much closer to the French King. He mounted the steps of the throne and presented the Sultan's letter in person. The French King and the Regent were also standing up during the reception. According to one French account,[59] the King had decided with the Regent that the same ceremonies observed for the audience of the French ambassador at the Porte would be applied. The King was to stay seated with his hat on while the nobility uncovered their heads. The Maréchal de Villeroi, whose status corresponded to that of the Grand Vezir who talked in the name of the Sultan during the audiences, would talk to Mehmed Efendi in the name of the King. Yet the young King stood up when Mehmed Efendi entered, thus committing a diplo-matic blunder.

The modes of Ottoman and French dress also differed. This difference was less visible in the Ottoman reception where the French ambassador and his retinue were each wearing a ceremonial robe presented before the audience to acknowledge symbolically their status before the Sultan. The French ambas-sador and his retinue were wearing their hats like the Ottoman officials. Mehmed Efendi's costumes contrasted with those of the French audience.

The portraits of Louis XV and Ahmed III epitomized the difference between the Ottoman and French modes of dress.[60] The long large caftan of the Ottoman Sultan contrasted with the tight-fitting costume of Louis XV. The Sultan also wore a large turban on his head covering all of his hair. Louis XV had long curly hair reaching his shoulders. The Sultan had a long beard unlike the King. Although the King was too young to have facial hair, beards had disappeared by the time of Louis XIV only to come back later.[61] The French King had a scepter which symbolized his power; the Ottoman Sultan

A portrait of the French King Louis XV. The painting is by Hyacinthe Rigaud (1659–1743); it is entitled "Louis XV (1710–1774) as a Child." (*From the Metropolitan Museum of Art, Purchase, Bequest of Mary Westmore Shively in memory of her husband, Henry L. Shively, M.D. 1960 (60.6); Photo by the Museum, all rights reserved*)

did not carry anything. These differences in costumes might explain the popular French interest in Mehmed Efendi and his retinue.

The size of the French and Ottoman reception halls also differed. The variation was evident in additional depictions of the French and Ottoman receptions. The French who had much larger audiences used vast reception

A miniature of the Ottoman Sultan Ahmed III and his son. Comparison with the preceding painting of Louis XV reveals cultural differences in clothing. The miniature is located in Topkapı Museum Library, Catalogue No. A3109. (*Courtesy of the Topkapı Palace Museum, Istanbul*)

halls in comparison to the Ottomans. The French halls had long corridors, high columns, and large windows; the King's throne dominated the hall. The Ottoman reception halls were much smaller in size. Most depictions of Ottoman receptions during the eighteenth century of various ambassadors by the Sultan and the Grand Vezir provided additional information on the use of space. In the receptions of ambassadors by the Grand Vezir, the physical distance between the ambassador and the vezir was less than that between the ambassador and the Sultan. The ambassador and his retinue stood around the vezir unaccompanied by Ottoman officials. The ambassador was also seated on a stool facing the seated vezir while the ambassador's retinue and a part of the vezir's household were standing. The room contained little or no furniture.

These Ottoman audiences with foreign ambassadors included a meal as well. The Ottoman officials all sat on the sofas around the room with the Grand Vezir at the center. The Grand Vezir usually had two translators on either side and the ambassador in front of him. The ambassador and his small retinue, all across from the sofa, were seated on small stools around the small low tables. This style of eating in small groups around tables emphasized the privacy the Ottomans attached to eating. The meal consisted of numerous courses rapidly served. The room had no fixed features as an eating room. Once the portable tables were moved, it could be used for any number of functions. These basic differences between the French and Ottoman receptions foreshadowed future differences between the French and Ottoman societies Mehmed Efendi was about to observe.

Manners

The main Ottoman-French difference emerged in drawing the boundaries of private and public life. The custom of disclosing living habits was totally new to the Ottomans. Ottomans spatially differentiated public and private spheres; the boundaries of the living unit were the private boundaries. The only living habit to be shared with and disclosed to people outside the household—and only close friends at that—was eating. Household members and a few close friends were the only people present at meals; foreigners were not usually invited to Ottoman houses until the Tulip Era. Among themselves, even the household members did not eat together; the women and men ate separately. Out of respect, the father of the household had the privilege to eat alone and was rarely joined by his sons even if they were old enough.[62] A French account of the eating manners of Mehmed Efendi and his retinue depicts that "even when his son sits with him, the son rises some time before his father out of respect."[63] The French, however, ate meals collectively with the participation of women. For the French, meals were the occasions to come together, talk, and socialize. The Ottomans ate in a very short period of time with haste and in total silence; European travelers were shocked by the speed with which the meals they had before their reception were served. For the French, eating took a long time; there was plenty of talking during the meal and hastening was a sign of disrespect.

Spatial arrangements for eating were also in accordance with the differences in eating habits. Ottomans did not have dining rooms.[64] Meals were served wherever the people were, usually in their living quarters, by valets who carried in the plates on a round tray and placed the tray on low stands. If a table was used, never more than six people crouched around it. No tablecloths, napkins, knives, forks, plates, or salt were present—there were only spoons. After going through thirty or forty small courses, people did not rise without cleaning their hands and faces. This was vastly different from the special dining rooms of the French. Meals were served to numerous people seated on chairs around a table. Napkins, forks, knives, numerous plates, and glasses were on the table. Wine was usually served during French meals whereas the Ottomans only consumed nonalcoholic fruit drinks after meals. Hence the whole approach to eating was different—privacy, respect, and a consequent silence dominated Ottoman eating manners, whereas entertainment and vivacity characterized the French. Various eighteenth-century miniatures and engravings portray these differences.[65]

As it evolved by the eighteenth century, the most important difference of the French meal from Ottoman meals was the presence of women. For a French meal, the room was lit by large ornate chandeliers and decorated by portraits. The large stationary table suggested that the uses of this room were restricted to eating. This table was especially structured to accommodate simultaneously all parties attending the meal. The seating arrangement enabled everyone to see and talk to each other. The meal was a social event for the French.

The long table covered with tablecloth and chairs around it gave the room and dining a permanence that was lacking in the Ottoman context. The candles, plates, spoons, forks, knives, and the variety of the courses present on the table enhanced the importance placed on the meal as a social gathering. The amount of care and attention put into the organization of the room and the table reflected the length of time spent at the meal. It took long hours, accompanied by wine and conversations.

As Braudel explains,[66] the luxury of these eating habits in France was a recent phenomenon. The table forks and flat plates that were preset on the table were sixteenth- and seventeenth-century luxuries. The spoon, used by the Ottomans for a long time, did not become widespread in the West until the sixteenth century. The table knives, forks, and glasses for each guest also

Ottoman meal during the reign of Sultan Ahmed III. The miniature is located in the Topkapı Museum Library, Catalogue No. A3593, folio 85b. (*Courtesy of the Topkapı Museum Library, Istanbul*)

French meal given by the Duke of Alva in 1707. Comparison with the preceding miniature reveals contrasts in Ottoman and French eating habits. The engraving is by G.I.B. Scotin Aine after that of Desmaretz; it is located in Bibliothèque de la Ville de Paris. (*Photo by Roger Viollet*)

dated from the sixteenth century. The luxury of a separate dining room evolved a century later; the nobleman now needed twice as many servants in the kitchen and in the dining room.

During Mehmed Efendi's visit, Mehmed Efendi mentioned the different eating manners. When the French wanted to watch the Ottomans eat, the Ottomans were shocked by this intrusion into their private lives. Mehmed Efendi, while noting this French request, took, however, the cultural differences into consideration:

> They wanted, in particular, to watch us eat. We received messages that the daughter of so-and-so or the wife of so-and-so requested permission to watch us eat. We could not always refuse. Since [our eating times] coincided with their fast, they would not eat but surround the dining table and watch us. Since we were not accustomed to such behavior, this distressed us very much. We endured with patience out of our consideration for them. Yet the French were accustomed to watching people eat; for example, it was their custom to permit some to watch their King eat. What was more strange was the fact that these people would go to watch the King rise and get dressed in the morning. The fact that they made similar requests of us made us very uneasy.[67]

Mehmed Efendi was obliged to give permission to the French to watch them eat when he was not able to free himself from them. Still, he stated that although being watched was embarrassing and unbearable for the Ottomans, the French were accustomed to the idea, and even watched their King sleep.[68]

Mehmed Efendi's accounts of the French King revealed how remote the Ottoman and French conceptions of royalty were from one another. Seriousness, sobriety, and gravity cloaked the Ottoman Sultan. The Sultan never revealed his emotions in audiences, kept his exchanges short, terse, and firm. He had to fulfill these requirements of his position regardless of his age. The court around him modeled their behavior after him. Mehmed Efendi's description of the French King and his court contrasted sharply with the Ottoman conception. After his public audience, Mehmed Efendi once saw the King at the palace. According to Mehmed Efendi, the King closely observed Mehmed Efendi's costume and dagger. A conversation between Mehmed Efendi and the King's tutor Villeroi followed.[69] The intimacy of this conversation could never have occurred in the Ottoman context. Mehmed Efendi narrated:

> He [Villeroi] asked, "What do you say about the beauty and grace of our King?" We replied, "Wonderful, may Allah protect him from evil eyes." He then held the King and turned him around. "He [the King] is only eleven years and four months old. Is he not well-proportioned with this stature? Particularly his hair is not a wig, look." We stroked and caressed those curly locks. . . . Then he (Villeroi) said, "His gait is also graceful. Walk some so they can see."

The King walked to the center of the hall like a dog and came back. "Let them see you run fast as well." The King jogged to the center of the hall and came back. The Marshal (Villeroi) asked if we liked it [the performance]. "May the Almighty Allah be praised for creating such a beautiful creature," we responded.

The informality of the King's tutor and the performance of the King could have never taken place in the Ottoman court, especially not in the presence of an ambassador. The foreign ambassadors were not even allowed to go anywhere near the living quarters of the Sultan. The living quarters in Ottoman society were accessible only to close family and friends. No Ottoman Sultan or official would even think of showing his living quarters or costumes to an ambassador the way the French King did to Mehmed Efendi.[70]

The Ottoman court would similarly behave with great reserve. Mehmed Efendi mentioned that he was once invited to a dance performance (which was actually a ballet) at the King's palace.[71] The dancers were "all the sons of princes, marshals, dukes, and other noblemen. In the King's court, these would always be the dancers." The close association of status and gravity excluded the possibility of such a performance in the Ottoman palace.

In spite of these vast differences between the two societies, Mehmed Efendi had no problems adapting to the French manners when necessary. When Marquis de Villeroi gave him a splendid dinner, Mehmed Efendi was seated with the French men and women of nobility and ate properly "à la française."[72] One particular aspect of French meals, namely drinking wine, was a habit Mehmed Efendi made a point of never exercising in public. His son occasionally drank wine, however. This strict observance on Mehmed Efendi's part derived from his position as the highest ranking Ottoman official. Yet he occasionally drank wine in private.[73] His escort la Beaune stated that Mehmed Efendi wanted some champagne and drank it with some of his principal officers, yet always moderately and without causing any embarrassment. Champagne, recently invented in France, was very fashionable.[74] Le Dran said Mehmed Efendi drank a few times, but always in private.

Even though wine drinking was forbidden in Islam, wine was consumed among the Ottomans. Yet the Ottomans used wine with great reserve in order not to harm their reputation in public.[75] Wine was not publicly consumed. Still, the flexible Ottoman attitude toward wine and its justification marks a deviation from Islamic mores. Ottoman Ahmet Bey's explanation to Lady Montagu about why he drank wine summarizes the Ottoman approach and justification of the issue:

Achmet Beg . . . made no scruple of deviating from some part of Mahomet's Law by drinking Wine with the same freedom we did. When I ask'd him how he came to allow himselfe that Liberty, he made Answer, all the Creatures of God were good and design'd for the use of Man; however, that the prohibition of Wine was a very wise maxim and meant for common people, being the Source of all disorders amongst them, but that the Prophet never design'd to confine those that knew how to use it with moderation; however, scandal ought to be avoided, and that he never drank it in public.[76]

Hence in the usage of wine, beside the public-private distinction for the sake of reputation, the common and the educated were also differentiated with respect to their consumption patterns. Commoners drank in excess causing damage, while educated men drank in moderation. Mehmed Efendi was very careful to observe this distinction as well. Even though he drank wine in moderation in private, he ordered that no one give wine to his retinue. Those of his retinue who went against his order were severely punished when, taking wine, they appeared drunk in public and committed a number of insolences.[77] In one case, when the Ottomans were invited to Versailles, it was gossiped that they speedily returned to Paris when four men in Mehmed Efendi's retinue, intoxicated, beat and wounded themselves with knife cuts, and one of them was found guilty of stealing a plate from the silver collection of the King.[78]

The problems Mehmed Efendi had with his retinue did not stop him from exercising a strict, private discipline over them. Mehmed Efendi regarded his retinue as his household and thus his family. If anyone in his retinue disobeyed, the punishment was at least fifty strokes of a stick with the number of strokes in proportion to the gravity of the offence. The blows were placed on the soles of the feet, and very rarely on the buttocks.[79] According to the accounts of la Beaune,[80] Mehmed Efendi's men were reasonable except the low domestics who were poorly disciplined—these men mutinied more than once and were punished. When la Beaune offered the services of his troops to control the mutiny, Mehmed Efendi refused, saying he could not accept the rule of a foreign authority over his family.

Mehmed Efendi's retinue was his household, a part of his private sphere of life. He accordingly required his men never to get involved in any public affairs. When the Ottomans were in Paris, the French musketeers started fighting among themselves in the quarter of the embassy, and a man from Mehmed Efendi's retinue tried to separate them by cudgelling. The quarrel turned itself onto the Ottoman who received a great sword thrust. Mehmed Efendi said that this incident did not concern him, and that he had told his men not to mingle in any public affair. This made the other men in his retinue very well-behaved. His conduct was strongly approved of by the French court.[81]

Although Mehmed Efendi had ordered his men not to mingle in any public affair, the mere presence of the Ottomans was a public affair in itself. The

French were very curious about the Ottomans and constantly wanted to catch a glimpse of them. The contrast between European uniformity and Ottoman plurality in costumes produced much of this interest. The Ottoman Empire was always full of people from different regions in different costumes and, accordingly, Europeans were always fascinated by Easterners; their curiosity was noted by most Ottoman travelers. Ahmed Azmi Efendi, the Ottoman ambassador to Berlin, often remarked on the curiosity of the Austrians during his voyage.[82] He tried not to stop at major cities because large crowds of people collected to watch him and blocked his way.

Similarly, Mehmed Efendi noted the French interest. He was astonished by the strange behavior of the French who traveled great distances and waited long hours just to see an Ottoman; the word he used for their curiosity was *hırs,* meaning avidity, eagerness, or covetousness.[83] Mehmed Efendi cited a number of incidents in relation to this French curiosity:[84]

> While we were on the canal, the desire of people to view us was such that they would make excursions from four or five-hour distances to the riverside to watch us. Striving to get in front of each other, they would fall into the water. . . . Being pressed by the crowd, the people would start crying out. Some women who entered our presence were unconscious. Although they had suffered terribly to enter, they would not leave the courtyard but wait expectantly for another chance. We marked some of them and witnessed their entrance three or four times with their thousand troubles. In cold and rainy weather, they would stand shivering in the courtyard until three or four o'clock at night. We were bewildered by their avidity (*hırs*).

The first cultural encounter of the Ottomans and the French thus took place as they evaluated each others' modes of living. Eating habits were different because of differences in defining private and public spheres, as mentioned previously. Mehmed Efendi redefined the public and private spheres in justifying his wine drinking and in disciplining his retinue. The last observed difference was in social behavior as the public curiosity of the French amazed the Ottomans.

Entertainment

One feature of European society that constantly startled the Ottomans was the participation of women in social life. Public deference shown to women in this participation was especially noted. All Ottomans as well as other Muslim visitors who had visited Europe made almost similar remarks about it.[85] On his visit to Vienna in 1665, Evliya Çelebi had stated:

When the king comes across a woman while on the road, if he is mounted, he stops his horse and lets the woman pass. If the king is on foot, he stops and joins his hands in front of him; the woman greets him and the king shows respect to her by taking off his hat. The king again lets the woman pass. In this land and other lands of the infidels, the word of say belongs to the women; women are so respected for the love of Virgin Mary.[86]

The fact that Europeans showed respect to women in this manner was difficult for the Ottomans to accept. Mehmed Efendi made one observation in which he seems to idealize the freedom and power women had:

> In France, esteem for women prevails among men. The women can do what they want and go where they desire. To the lowest, the best gentleman would show more regard and respect than necessary. In these lands, women's commands are enforced. So much so that France is the paradise of women. They have no hardships or troubles at all—it is said that they obtain their wishes and desires without any resistance whatsoever.[87]

Evliya's observation was solely about public participation of women. Mehmed Efendi also took the public participation of women into consideration when he estimated the population of Paris. He stated that, unlike Constantinople where women rarely wandered in the streets,[88] Paris seemed crowded because women never stayed in their houses and went around visiting house by house, increasing the number of people on the streets. Mehmed Efendi also dealt with the social participation of women. He tried to assess the role of women in society and was successful since he participated in social life, unlike Evliya Çelebi.

Mehmed Efendi had frequent associations with French women. On his way to Paris,[89] Mehmed Efendi politely received ladies, seated them on chairs, and presented them with coffee and fruit preserves. He asked them to remove their gloves and commented that he had never seen such beautiful hands. When in Paris, women of the court and the city came to visit him.[90] Mehmed Efendi engaged in gallant conversation with them through the interpreter and returned their visits. He was very popular with French women because he showered them with praises and compliments. Mehmed Efendi used almost every occasion for a compliment. When asked by a number of the visiting ladies why he did not bring any of his wives to Paris,[91] beside noting the difficulty of the voyage, Mehmed Efendi stated that "he was persuaded he would find in France ladies all more beautiful and witty than all those he could have been able to bring from Constantinople." In another instance, when the lady sitting next to him at the ballet inquired about his impressions of the ballet, he responded "her charms occupied him so much that he had not been able to pay attention to the ballet.''[92] Another lady, who had been the wife of Monsieur Girardin, the former French ambassador to the Porte, gave a party in Mehmed Efendi's honor one night. She dressed up in an Ottoman dress and had food served in the Ottoman style. Mehmed Efendi was ''astonished by the singular attention of the lady and made great praises.''[93] Mehmed Efendi had no difficulty in adapting to the social participation of women although the Ottoman women remained within the boundaries of private life. He applied his experience in associating with Ottoman women in the private sphere to the French women in the public sphere.

The vast difference between the private and public lives of Ottoman women in the eighteenth century was portrayed by some European painters. The Ottoman women, when resting in their private quarters with closed heavy curtains, wore low-cut dresses. Most were seated comfortably on the floor, attending to a variety of functions. One made coffee on the brazier heating up the room while another served food into bowls on a low table. Some chatted with each other while a few took care of a baby in a cradle. A rare appearance of the Ottoman women in public space revealed the vast difference between the positions of women in private and public. The appearance of the women totally changed; their bodies and faces were heavily covered. Such distinction as existed between the private and public lives of Ottoman women permeated Ottoman society.

The vast disparity between public and private spheres of life in the Ottoman and French societies was not the only difference Mehmed Efendi encountered. Some forms of entertainment, such as the opera, ballet, and concerts, were totally outside Mehmed Efendi's cultural experience. The Ottomans had been used to public festivities and plays as the only forms of entertainment.[94] Public festivities occurred for specific reasons like the birth of a prince, a court marriage, the departure for a new conquest, or the arrival of a welcome foreign ambassador or guest. These were all one-time occasions. Only in the eighteenth century did Ahmed III establish a secular fête called the Tulip fête to amuse courtiers and others and to impress the world by displaying his magnificence. The Ottoman performances were not as frequent as the French ones to which Mehmed Efendi was invited.

Qualitative differences existed as well. Ottoman performances concurrently included processions, illuminations, fireworks, equestrian games, and hunting as well as dancing, music, and poetic recitations. They resembled country fairs. The French operas, ballets, and concerts, however, were performed in settings specially constructed for these events, were limited to a particular audience, and provided occasions for social gatherings and interactions. Ottoman plays, the only performances somewhat similar to the French, were not performed in special buildings and did not rely on scenery. They were performed everywhere:

> a raised platform was never used as a stage by these performers. . . . The play had little or no action, depending for its laughter on lively slapstick and on monologue or dialogue involving puns, ready wit, a quick response, crude practical jokes, double meanings, misunderstandings, and interpolated quips. . . . Everything was done to music.[95]

There was no adherence to a specific text as in the French plays. This was Mehmed Efendi's experience before he saw French opera, ballet, and concerts.

Miniatures and engravings from the eighteenth century portrayed the differences between Ottoman and French entertainments.[96] The French theatre was set on a stage, with the frequent accompaniment of an orchestra. The stage was away from the audience; there was a clear-cut separation between viewers and performers. Ottoman public entertainment involved a number of actors who performed while the viewers stood by watching them. The setting for the Ottoman entertainment was much more informal. Mehmed Efendi was about to encounter a setting different from the one he had been used to.

The cultural context and its impact on the reception of such a new observation was evident in the case of the Persian ambassador Mehmed Rıza Bey who was in Paris in 1706, fourteen years before Mehmed Efendi. When Mehmed Rıza Bey went to the opera,[97] a special place had to be furnished for him in the middle of the amphitheater with cushions and a mattress. He sat there and smoked through the opera, drinking coffee and tea. After the opera, he invited two of the lady dancers to his house, offering them sable furs for their trouble. Mehmed Rıza Bey perceived the opera as a private spectacle and did not have any concern for the context within which the performance took place.

Mehmed Efendi, however, was more observant. He and his retinue were seated as the rest of the French and behaved like them. The French recorded the reactions of the Ottomans. Buvat stated that "Mehmed Efendi seemed so charmed that they saw him make without cessation gestures of the head and the hands. One of his officers was not able to prevent himself from laughing during the whole performance"[98]—a breach of Ottoman "gravitas." The opera Mehmed Efendi initially attended was *Thesée*,[99] a lyric tragedy of Quinault, music by Lully. Mehmed Efendi defined the opera ("opare" as he called it) as a play particular to the French where they showed strange arts. He remarked that the building had been specially constructed, and the seats were hierarchically allocated. He then described the illuminated stage as the curtain rose:

After everyone took their place, the curtain was raised suddenly and a great palace appeared behind it. In the courtyard of the palace, dancers in their special dresses, and about twenty fairy-like figures appeared in their jeweled costumes bringing splendor to the gathering. They started singing a song together with the instruments. After dancing for a while, they started the opera. The object of this [opera] is to play a story. The French have made each story into a book and printed it. In all, there were thirty books. Each one had a name. In each gathering, they displayed one story as if it were just happening. . . . They performed the love situation to such a degree that one would start to feel compassion just by watching the gestures of the sultan, his son, and the girl.[100]

The aspects of the opera that drew Mehmed Efendi's attention were those he had not been accustomed to. The most important was the change of scenery during the opera since the Ottoman performances had no set scenery at all. The plot and the literary tradition behind it were also different and therefore noteworthy. Acting also drew Mehmed Efendi's attention. Since the performers imitated different people and never identified themselves with one character in the Ottoman plays, Mehmed Efendi was affected by the passion with which the actors and actresses played their parts.

Mehmed Efendi stated that two days later he "was invited to an opera gathering at the Kings' palace."[101] The performance Mehmed Efendi saw was different from opera and concentrated mainly on dancing, but he perceived it as an opera since that was the only similar event he had seen, and the only context to which he could refer. The French contemporaries referred to it as a ballet.[102]

The Ottoman perceptions of these distinctions gradually developed as interaction with the West continued. Ahmed Azmi Efendi was the Ottoman ambassador to Berlin sixty years after Mehmed Efendi. He did not describe the opera at all, but simply referred to their having been invited to "the houses of shadow play."[103] He did not need to describe this experience; by then opera was incorporated into the Ottoman cultural framework as one sort of shadow play.

French music, frequently used in these performances, was also different from Ottoman music. Rather than explaining the difference, Mehmed Efendi stated that numerous musicians, during meals, played instruments that he had not seen. He also did not mention either the concerts he attended[104] or the concert that was supposed to be given on oriental music (unclear as to whether by the King's musicians or Mehmed Efendi's).[105] Mehmed Efendi only noted the organ he listened to at the Chapel of the Invalides.[106] The extent of his interest in the organ was mentioned by d'Aubigny,[107] who stated that Mehmed Efendi had promised to introduce the organ in Constantinople. On his return, Mehmed Efendi sent an Ottoman musician to Paris to study that

Theatre presented at the Versailles. The engraving is from a book entitled *Fêtes de Versailles*, which is located in the Topkapı Museum Library, Catalogue No. H2587. All the engravings in the book have attached explanations in Ottoman. The attached Ottoman explanation on this particular engraving can be translated as "dance plays performed during the feast given at the Versailles." (*Courtesy of the Topkapı Museum Library, Istanbul*)

instrument. Another event also not mentioned by Mehmed Efendi was a discourse on music.[108] The differences between oriental music and French and Italian music were discussed. Mehmed Efendi, appearing very knowledgeable about Ottoman music, confessed that French music charmed him more. This revelation, either out of politeness or personal preference, may indicate that he had been sufficiently initiated in French music.

All these French performances revealed how qualitatively different Ottoman and French notions of entertainment were. Quantitative differences, however, evolved around the frequency of performances. The Ottomans had infrequent entertainments in comparison to the French. Although Mehmed

Ottoman entertainment scene during the reign of Ahmed III. The miniature is located in the Topkapı Museum Library, Catalogue No. A3594, folio 87a. (*Courtesy of the Topkapı Museum Library, Istanbul*)

Efendi's situation as a special ambassador may have caused him to be entertained constantly, when compared to the Ottoman entertainment provided for foreign ambassadors, the French outnumbered the Ottomans. The reason for this quantitative difference was pointed out by Ahmed Azmi Efendi.[109] On being invited to the palace of a count, he complained

> it is a strange habit of Europeans that . . . nobody remembers and considers where [a notable man from other lands] will stay and how he will support himself during his stay. They just immediately detain him from his road asking him to stay in their city for a few days for sightseeing. They then take pride in themselves by bringing the traveler just to the banquets they give each other and they claim to have shown honor to the visitor.

In the Ottoman Empire, the only receptions foreign ambassadors attended were given solely in their honor; ambassadors were not generally invited to the feasts Ottomans gave each other. The French, however, considered the receptions they gave each other as social events and freely invited the ambassadors to each and every one. In the end, the French spent more time entertaining themselves and the ambassadors than the Ottomans did.

The French patterns of entertainment had also changed during the time of Louis XV. Under Louis XV, "the center of gravity of entertainment shifted from the palaces to the residences of non-princely aristocrats."[110] Mehmed Efendi was in Paris during this shift which vastly increased the number of parties, the number of people attending them, and the duration of the entertainment.

Nighttime entertainment became very fashionable as well. Because many artifical light shows took place at night, Mehmed Efendi was impressed by the fireworks.[111] The frequent artificial light shows in Paris were majestic, unlike the rare Ottoman fireworks.[112] The French light show produced a majestic effect because of its scale and its coordination. All the lights were synchronized to go on simultaneously. The audience watched the spectacle from a distance as if viewing a theatre performance. Ottoman fireworks were performed in a totally different setting. Different fireworks were lit by different people at different times. The audience, consisting, in addition to the Palace household and officials, of the city populace standing closeby, was separated from the fireworks by soldiers. The Ottoman nighttime entertainment was an ongoing show rather than one big spectacle.

The Ottomans and the French had different organizations of time as well. The Ottomans divided the days according to prayer hours. There were no public clocks—time was organized around calls to prayer five times a day. Daily public life began with the prayer at daybreak and dwindled with the prayer at dusk. The cities were not lit because "the mores of the nation

Artificial light show on the Versailles canal. The engraving is from the book *Fêtes de Versailles*, which is located in the Topkapı Museum Library, Catalogue No. H2587. The attached Ottoman explanation can be translated as "the firework show at the basin and its vicinity located in the Versailles garden." (*Courtesy of the Topkapı Museum Library, Istanbul*)

rendered that precaution useless: no one went out at night."[113] This was completely different from the French temporal organization in which Mehmed Efendi participated. The French seemed to utilize the day on a twenty-four hour basis. The balls lasted well into the early morning hours.[114] Although Mehmed Efendi did not mention it, he attended a masked ball that continued until six in the morning.[115]

Ottoman nighttime entertainment scene during the reign of Sultan Ahmed III. The miniature is located in the Topkapı Museum Library, Catalogue No. A3593, folio 34a. (*Courtesy of the Topkapı Museum Library, Istanbul*)

In all, the performances Mehmed Efendi encountered in Paris were cultur-ally different from the Ottoman performances from a number of perspectives. Qualitatively, they were organized in special settings that were not familiar to him. Quantitatively, Mehmed Efendi attended more performances than he could have in Constantinople because the rationale behind giving receptions was different. The French organization of time differed as well; the Ottomans slept while the French were still enjoying themselves yet started the day earlier than the French.[116]

There was one shared French and Ottoman pastime: hunting. Mehmed Efendi discussed the hunts he had been invited to at length. In one with the King, various birds and rabbits were freed to be hunted. Mehmed Efendi said they enjoyed themselves for three or four hours.[117] He was also invited to a deer hunt at Chantilly.[118] Since Mehmed Efendi could associate his prior experiences with this activity, he said he was gratified by the hunting.

Art and Architecture

Ottoman and French palaces, houses, and gardens differed in both their exte-rior and interior designs. The Ottomans, in general, were "not at all solicitous to beautify the outsides of their houses; they built their houses quickly out of wood."[119] The beautifully proportioned public buildings were an exception to this pattern. The houses were erected for functional purposes and did not outwardly display the wealth of the owner. Display of luxury in any sphere of life, including architecture, was not considered proper by the tenets of Islam. Nothing was simpler than the construction of a house for the Ottomans. Their houses were usually not more than one or two stories, very rarely three.[120] Foreigners claimed that telling one Ottoman house from another was difficult since all were built irregularly without distinctive features. When The Euro-peans viewed an Ottoman house, being unable to distinguish either a front or wings, they labeled the whole building a total confusion.[121] The house was built without any planned spatial organization and nor with any concern for orderliness or coherence in using materials or space. The gardens, harmo-nious with the rest of the house, consisted of "arbors, fountains, and walks thrown together in agreeable confusion."[122]

Despite this entangled appearance on the outside, internally the houses were very simply decorated.[123] Floors were covered by carpets. The principal pieces of furniture of the house were sofas with many cushions. Sofas served the functions of couches and chairs which were not known or used in the East. Meals were served on a tray placed on a portable low stand. At night, candles were set on small tables to provide light, and people slept on sofas. During the day, things were stored in closets or wooden chests located in each room.

Recesses between the closets on the walls were used as cupboards. Not many accessories were in the house except for an occasional portable mirror brought from Venice and porcelain from China.

Constantinople, the capital of the Ottoman Empire, reflected this architectural composition. Western travelers were often struck by the diversity of the environment. Chevalier de Camilly, who escorted Mehmed Efendi back, drew a very vivid picture of Constantinople. He portrayed the city as a large amphitheater:

> It was, to my pleasure, the most magnificent view which there could be in the world, to view on one side His Highness at the center of his pages, his guards, his janissaries, and the other dignitaries of his court, all dressed in loud and odd colors, with extraordinary headgears. [And] to view on the other side those prodigious quantities of houses, mosques, minarets which cover the slopes of the two steep mountains which border the port of Constantinople. All together form one large amphitheater which appears to be constructed to give all the universe the portrayal of one of those naval battles which the ancients called "mock sea-fights" (naumachies).[124]

The mystic charm and the challenge provided by the diversity and contrasts among the sites can be easily visualized in this quotation.

Paris presented another form of visual organization to Mehmed Efendi. His description focused on the specific differences between Paris and Constantinople in construction:[125]

> The city of Paris, in reality, is not as large as Constantinople. Yet its houses have three or four floors, and many have seven floors. On each floor, an entire family resides. The number of people on the streets seem more than actual since the women never stay home and are continually on the streets. . . . Its shops are curious and filled with rarities.

Mehmed Efendi was correct in his population estimate. The city of Paris had approximately 450,000 inhabitants during the first decades of the eighteenth century.[126] The population estimate for Constantinople with the suburbs in the seventeenth century was between 700,000 and 800,000.[127] The expansion patterns of the two cities were different. Istanbul, like Islamic cities in general, "had low houses clustered together like pomegranate seeds."[128] The city grew horizontally into the suburbs. The situation was different in the West. The city grew vertically as new stories were added to the buildings. Most buildings were being built with brick toward the end of the seventeenth century.[129]

Mehmed Efendi made a number of comments on external constructions of palaces and gardens. The palace he saw at Chambord was "similar to a censer with six domes and its handiwork is as delicate as that of a table clock. . . .

One has to see it in order to give a just description."[130] As Mehmed Efendi got nearer Paris, he gave more descriptions of the palaces; they were constructed in "a manner new to him."[131] When he saw St. Cloud, Meudon, and Versailles, one common theme in all his descriptions involved the gardens and their designs: water fountains, cascades, canals, and statues. The orderliness of the gardens and the care the French showed toward their gardens were also remarkable to Mehmed Efendi. He observed that the French had built "walls from trees and plants." After riding through these long roads surrounded by green walls, he was surprised to see how much work was put into "maintaining just a piece of the forest every year."[132] French palaces and gardens were exhilarating for Mehmed Efendi. He could observe and explain them easily; they could also be effectively copied in Constantinople.

Mehmed Efendi also described the menageries in the gardens in great detail. For instance, at Chantilly, in buildings especially constructed for animals, Mehmed Efendi saw a llama for the first time. He described it as an animal from the New World with "claws like those of deer, a body as large as that of oxen, and hair resembling that of sheep. Its neck is as long as that of a horse and its ears are likewise similar to a horse's ears, whereas its head, mouth, nose, and eyes are like those of a deer."[133] However, the parrots squawking in French seemed to affect him most.

The difference in internal spatial construction between the French and the Ottomans caused special difficulties for Mehmed Efendi and his retinue. When under quarantine at Sete in an old church, Mehmed Efendi had to ask for a room filled with water closets to be emptied out to make room for a common gathering place; he said they needed a large gathering place more than water closets. The people in Mehmed Efendi's retinue also wanted a place for their baths. The French complied with the requests and designed Mehmed Efendi's lodgings in Paris accordingly. Mehmed Efendi himself very rarely commented on French internal decoration. When visiting Versailles, he stated that the French were accustomed to covering the walls of their rooms with a piece of rug or other velvet-like fabrics. When in the Galerie des Glaces, he observed that the windows opening to the garden and the use of mirrors made the room appear very large and bright.[134]

Paintings and textiles were significant in revealing how Mehmed Efendi emphasized those products already in his cultural framework and ignored those out of it. Since paintings hanging on walls were not a familiar part of the Ottoman cultural framework, Mehmed Efendi did not pay attention to and was not impressed with the paintings exhibited at the palace. For the Ottomans, paintings existed only in book illustrations. Mehmed Efendi just stated he saw some "wonderful, amazing depictions"[135] hung at the galleries. The palace certainly contained many remarkable paintings of the time.

This passing reference of Mehmed Efendi indicated his disinterest in paintings. The disinterest could have originated from his Muslim sensibilities; Islam does not view depictions of human figures favorably.

Yet Mehmed Efendi's reaction to some other human figures he saw on textiles in a textile workhouse refutes this explanation. So, the disinterest was cultural, not religious. Mehmed Efendi did not lack aesthetic sensitivity; it was channeled to a different area than painting. However, Mehmed Efendi carefully described the textiles he saw as if they were paintings. He defined the tapestry (Gobelin) factory as "a workhouse for *kilim* weavers."[136] The expressiveness of the human figures on these textiles impressed him. Mehmed Efendi showed his appreciation of this expressiveness by comparing them to an Ottoman cultural product, miniatures:

> In their portrayals, the looks, eyelashes, eyebrows, and especially their hair and beards were presented to such a degree that even Mani and Bihzad [two celebrated miniaturists] would have been unable to perform as well on Chinese paper. In some figures, sadness shows sorrow, in others, fright shows fear; some weeping figures, other suffering figures have been so well portrayed that everyone's condition can be understood at first glance.

Mehmed Efendi's enthusiasm persisted when he encountered the familiar context of looms. A lengthy discussion about the kinds of thread used, and how the designs were sketched on cloth and then embroidered followed. Mehmed Efendi also visited looms in Lyon that specialized in brocades, silk velvets, and velvets.[137]

Within the cultural field of art and architecture, Mehmed Efendi encountered a spectrum of Western products ranging from palaces, houses, and gardens to furniture. Paintings were excluded from the Ottoman cultural framework by religion, so Mehmed Efendi regarded them as uninteresting. Textile workhouses and looms were within the Ottoman experience and therefore stimulating.

Science and Technology

Mehmed Efendi was especially careful in describing scientific developments since he had been sent specifically to observe science and technology. The developments Mehmed Efendi focused on were mainly in two fields: the military, consisting of maneuvers and hospital for veterans, and scientific, involving the observatory, mirror factory, and the museum of natural history.

Ottomans needed and wanted to apply these developments in the Ottoman Empire yet failed to do so. The decline in Ottoman military efficiency and organization had become evident by the number of defeats the army had begun to suffer. In science, the Ottoman Empire had been in a steady decline since the seventeenth century. In the schools, courses in canonical jurisprudence had gradually gained importance over the rational and positive sciences.[138] Medical schools also started to decline in the seventeenth century and their inefficiency resulted in the spread of apprenticeship practices. The state had to issue orders to control practitioners without certificates; these unqualified people were causing great damage to the populace.[139]

The description of French science and technology by Mehmed Efendi presented a totally different picture. The French displayed the excellent condition of their army in the exhibitions to which Mehmed Efendi was invited. During the military maneuvers, Mehmed Efendi was impressed by the discipline of the army which, on every command, was able to change positions as one body.[140] The inventiveness of the French defense was reflected in the one hundred and twenty-five models of forts and fortifications Mehmed Efendi was shown.[141] These models allowed for the study of the landscape from all directions to predict the path of enemy attack and to take precautions against it. Mehmed Efendi added that all the expense for building these miniature representations was worthwhile. The hospital for veterans symbolized the good maintenance of the French army.[142] As Mehmed Efendi went through the hospital, he noted the cleanliness of the five or six hundred beds and the physicians present with all the necessary equipment. The tour ended with an inspection of the bakery, kitchen, and dining halls, all of which also reflected cleanliness and order.

The military maneuvers Mehmed Efendi saw illustrated a new discipline imposed by technological improvement of armaments and warfare. Castle reliefs used new measuring and scaling techniques. The veteran's hospital was also the product of a welfare network absent from Ottoman society.

Mehmed Efendi observed many notable technological developments as well. He spent a lot of time at the observatory, surveying, for the first time in his life, the planets of Venus, Saturn, Jupiter, and the moon through a telescope. His astronomical descriptions cover a substantial portion of his embassy account.[143] Mehmed Efendi became interested in the observatory because it was the month of Ramazan and he wanted to know if the new moon was out yet. Upon visiting the observatory, he was very enthusiastic in describing the telescope:

> The French have produced a field glass to observe the fixed stars and the planets. It is as follows: they have mounted a mirror like that of a barber's on something like a well pump. They have laid inside that a ship's sail more than fifty arms' (*zira'*) long. They then placed a smaller mirror inside the top of the field glass. In all, it has two mirrors. Placing a thick pole of a ship's sail upon an elevated spot in the observatory, they suspended the instrument by attaching a

pulley-like wheel to the top of the pole. They have tied one end of that instrument to the field glass and have suspended pieces of lead and iron from the other end.[144]

As Mehmed Efendi kept observing, his descriptions became more vivid. He identified the moon looking like spongy bread (*içi süngerlenmiş somun ekmeği*), and prayed every time he saw a new satellite as predicted by the French. Mehmed Efendi was also aware of the role played by the monarch in encouraging scientific progress; he attributed French progress to the benevolence of the King. As a souvenir, he was presented with the astronomical tables of Uluğ Bey which Cassini had improved. This observatory was technologically far beyond the Ottoman achievements. The mirror factory presented a popularized application of advanced technology. Mehmed Efendi visited the royal mirror factory which contained one thousand workers and approximately two hundred workbenches.

The wide base on which the French founded their technological development became evident through Mehmed Efendi's account of the museum of natural history.[145] He saw the sections on anatomy, medicine, and plants. In the anatomy section, beside the dissections of beasts and birds, ''there were dissections of several men, women, and children whose every organ could be observed. Each organ had been exactly reproduced from wax revealing the flesh, the fat, the arteries, and the nerves.'' Mehmed Efendi was presented with two wax anatomies of an animal and a man.[146] The plants grown in artificial gardens were a totally new sight for Mehmed Efendi. He said these plants were ''preserved in winter quarters like greenhouses which were surrounded by glass frames and which had furnaces and metal sheets to control the heat and the moisture.'' This must have been a new concept for the Ottomans since the corresponding Ottoman word *ser* did not exist at the time and was presumably adopted after this embassy from the French ''serre.''

Out of these technological developments the cultivation and preservation of plants were easily introduced to the Ottoman Empire. The institutional setting for sciences that could absorb, apply, and advance these scientific advancements was not yet ready. This institutional setting came into being only as scientific knowledge diffused into Ottoman society through education.

Mehmed Efendi did not mention the libraries he visited and the books he saw. He just stated that the many interesting sites and libraries he observed were beyond explanation. The French accounts,[147] however, described his visit to the Royal Library. Mehmed Efendi stayed there until seven at night astonished by the quantity of Ottoman and Arabic manuscripts, Qur'ans, and other rare books in their collection. He appeared to have ample knowledge of history and rare books. The manuscripts on the history of the Bible enriched with miniatures depicting the creation of the world and the New Testament were, however, new to him. As a gift, he was given the ancient Latin edition of all the printed works of Aristotle.[148] According to Saint Simon, Mehmed Efendi stated that ''he was a particular friend of the Grand Vezir, and, on his return, he was going to propose to him the establishment of an Ottoman printing press and a library in spite of the aversion of the Turks.''[149] His son was to be successful in this endeavor.

Gift Exchange

The exchange of gifts was a regularly observed custom in international relations. The nature of the gift reflected the idealized values of the presenting and receiving societies. The value of the gift was determined by the status and prestige considerations of the two societies as well as the gift's political expediency and purpose. Description of the gifts threw some light on the economic conditions, regional products, and relative wealth and industrial development of the two societies.[150] The gift exchange between Mehmed Efendi and the French King can be analyzed within this format.[151] The Ottoman gifts represented objects regarded important by Ottoman society. They concerned hunting or war, corresponding to a life based on traveling and war filled with tents, horse harnesses, and weapons. These objects also carried marks of luxury and richness; they were studded with precious stones. Gifts Mehmed Efendi brought the French emphasized equitation and warfare equipment like horses, bows, and a sabre. There were also fine materials such as silk, muslin, brocade, Indian clothes; clothing like fur coats; and numerous bottles of Mecca balm. The Mecca balm reflected the assumptions the Ottomans made about the French. At the time, this balm was believed to have magical healing powers so the Ottomans assumed the gift would be in demand and therefore welcome.

Gifts of the Europeans, however, consisted mainly of textiles, richly ornamented clothing, goldsmith's work, and chandeliers. European societies indicated a high regard for technological products by the nature of their gifts and viewed these products as the prominent objects of their culture. Gifts given to Mehmed Efendi by the King included such technological products as pendules, watches, and mirrors; cultural products such as chests of drawers (commodes), dressing cases (nécessaires), and desks (bureaus) hitherto not used by the Ottomans. Since pictures were not permissible in Islam, the French gave, at the ambassador's request, a diamond studded belt instead of a portrait of the French king encrusted with diamonds.[152] Precious weapons such as pistols and guns were also presented to the Ottomans because of the high Ottoman regard for weapons.

Twenty years after this initial gift exchange, the son of Mehmed Efendi,

Mehmed Said Efendi, went to Paris as an ambassador. The gifts of Mehmed Said Efendi were standard; they either concentrated on equitation material such as armor, saddles, stirrups, sabres, or on traditional military weapons like pistols, guns, and daggers. The collection of French gifts to Mehmed Said Efendi indicated the increasing diversity in taste among the Ottomans. A chandelier and a round dinner table for twelve persons were presented. Being aware of Ottoman eating customs, however, the French had modified the table by adding a large centerpiece that could contain as many as forty bowls—to hold the large variety of dishes the Ottomans consumed during their meals. Additional mirrors and a microscope as gifts reflected continued French technological superiority and Ottoman interest. As Mehmed Efendi reported on various aspects of French civilization ranging from different forms of entertainment to new architectural forms to scientific advances, he was stretching the parameters of the French impact on Ottoman society.

3

The Return

Il (Mehmed Efendi) est le premier des Turcs qui ait osé donner à la Porte une idée convenable de la grandeur et de la puissance de nos rois. . . . Les Turcs sont si remplis de leur grandeur et les oreilles de leur princes sont si délicates qu'on trouva extraordinaire et même surprenant que Mehemet efendi eût osé parler des beautés de la France et de la magnificence de notre cour dans les terms qu'il a fait, dans un écrit qui devait être vu par son maître. Ceux qui l'ont vue et dont la vanité en a été offensée se sont dédommagés en disant que c'était des contes faits à plaisir.[1]

Mehmed Efendi's account ended with a short summary of his trip back to Constantinople; he briefly mentioned the names of the villages, towns, and cities on his land route from Paris to Montpellier, concluding with the names of the islands (and Tunisia) which they stopped by on the sea route from Montpellier to Constantinople. He did not provide much information about his return to Constantinople. Contemporary French accounts, however, give detailed information about the events surrounding his return and his reception in Constantinople. Two French vessels commanded by the Chevaliers de Camilly and de Nangis brought Mehmed Efendi back to Constantinople.

Mehmed Efendi left a very good impression on the French. The King treated him exceptionally, receiving him very often. Usually, the ambassadors from the East did not see the King on any occasions other than the public audience.[2] Louis XV must have liked the company of the Ottoman ambassador. The contemporary French accounts of Mehmed Efendi were also very favorable. One such account noted how someone from such a different society could have such an enlightened curiosity and European taste:

> That minister from the Orient has shone in all his manner with a European taste. He has visited all the places that are sought by an enlightened curiosity, has surveyed all cabinets of curiosities, and has leafed through select libraries. In all, he had a strong understanding of the customs and manners of our nation: our

nation has rendered justice to his merit, and he has proved that our nation should never judge people by the climate and by habits of life.[3]

The embassy to Paris affected Mehmed Efendi and his retinue very favorably as well—perhaps too favorably: contemporary French accounts stated that there were desertions in France from Mehmed Efendi's retinue.[4] Mehmed Efendi was abandoned by at least three of his men. One was his "Jewish attendant Moise"[5] whose desertion greatly upset Mehmed Efendi since Moise had taken advantage of his closeness to remove and sell part of his master's goods. Moise, a member of the Jewish minority in the Ottoman Empire, could have found the conditions in France more amenable. Mehmed Efendi wrote a letter to Duc d'Orleans asking him to surrender Moise. The Duc replied that a search had been ordered but remained fruitless since Moise, dressed up as a Frenchman, could not be traced.

The other man who left Mehmed Efendi's retinue converted to Christianity. He has been traced by a French naturalization permit given to a certain Louis Ovanete of Longy in 1745 who was

> a native of Constantinople, practicing the profession of apostolic and Roman Catholic religion . . . who had come to France in the year 1721, with the suite of the Turkish ambassador and had been, by our orders and care, elevated into the Catholic religion. He has served for a number of years in our troops as a lieutenant of the Infantry, and had married in our city of Versailles in the month of November 1721, and is now resolved to remain in our Kingdom and end his days here.[6]

The third man was "a cook, Meckmet." Dubois took this "Turkish convert who was a pastry cook" into his service.[7] The accounts stated that Mehmed Efendi became much more severe with his retinue after these desertions and wanted to wait a few more days in France with the hope that these men would return.

There were also a few French who attempted to join Mehmed Efendi's retinue. One day rumor ran that the daughter of a physician at Versailles had dressed herself up as a man and slipped into Mehmed Efendi's suite.[8] At Fontainebleau, while reviewing the Ottoman equipment, the translator la Beaune discovered hidden a young man who, lured by the excitement of a voyage to the East, had dressed up as a Turk. The man was immediately arrested and imprisoned. Suspicions about French people joining the retinue continued and French officials noted they would do all they could to stop the embarkation of any French deserters.[9]

According to French accounts, the embarkation for Constantinople itself caused numerous problems in addition to those resulting from the desertions.[10] Mehmed Efendi had brought one-hundred-ninety quintals of coffee from Constantinople to sell at a profit in Paris.[11] He most probably did make a large profit since coffee had become a public consumption item in the West but was not yet available in large quantities. The comparative advantage of Arabian coffee persisted until the second half of the eighteenth century.[12] With the money from the sale of this coffee, Mehmed Efendi purchased sixty to seventy bales of cloth. He most probably purchased this cloth in Lyon where he visited cloth manufacturers.[13] In Lyon, the men in Mehmed Efendi's retinue purchased "considerable numbers of firearms, and silk, silver, and gold-threaded fabrics."[14] The Chevalier de Camilly in charge of the ships told Mehmed Efendi he could not embark all the merchandise since there was not sufficient space in the ships. Camilly suggested sending the merchandise, without freight charge, by ships that left every day for Constantinople. Mehmed Efendi declared that he would not leave if the merchandise were not with him. All the merchandise was embarked. In Constantinople, Mehmed Efendi sold the cloth at a cheaper rate than the French tradesmen, briefly undermining the French trade.[15]

Finances had always been a problem during the journey although Mehmed Efendi never mentioned them in his account. He no doubt expected, like some later Ottoman ambassadors to Europe, reciprocal privileges—the same sort of lavish hospitality received by European ambassadors in Istanbul. Mehmed Efendi was duly disappointed. During the voyage, he claimed that the nine hundred livres given for himself, fifty livres for his son, and fifty for his attendant were not enough. He consequently refused to pay for his lodgings at Montpellier and Sète, and the French captains had to buy provisions during the sea voyage.[16] Still, Mehmed Efendi seemed to be in financial difficulties; he wanted to borrow thirteen thousand francs from la Beaune to pay his men.[17] Mehmed Efendi said he would return the money once he sold some coffee in Paris. Although there was no indication as to whether he was given this amount or not, Lenoir the translator claimed he had lent ten thousand francs to Mehmed Efendi and wanted to take possession of Mehmed Efendi's belongings. The French dissuaded Lenoir from taking action.[18] None of these financial difficulties were mentioned by Mehmed Efendi although similar problems were later noted by Ottoman ambassadors to Berlin and Madrid.

Some aspects of his embassy were not mentioned in Mehmed Efendi's account for a number of reasons. The first was due to the nature of embassy reports. Embassy reports were either private or general.[19] Private reports were political documents stating how the actual mission was carried out. They were functional rather than ceremonial. General reports, however, were those documenting all the ambassador had been able to learn about the social and administrative life, military condition, culture, and civilization level of the host country. There were no interpretations of the ambassador added to the report. After reading Mehmed Efendi's initial report, Bonnac stated that "he (Mehmed Efendi) well noted many of the things he saw and described almost all with much exactitude . . . but it is surprising that he has never said anything either on the subject of his embassy, or on the spirit of the (French) nation, nor on the characteristics of the diverse persons with whom he had dealt. For all intents and purposes, his account is of material things."[20] Although Bonnac was disillusioned, it was precisely the fact of his being able to read the report that limited its political content—it was not confidential. Mehmed Efendi was not likely to say anything of political significance in a report that received such widespread circulation.[21]

Mehmed Efendi seems to have given a very detailed private oral report to the Sultan and the Grand Vezir. This can be detected from the French accounts during and after Mehmed Efendi's voyage. In his account,[22] while describing the military maneuver he had reviewed with the King, Mehmed Efendi skipped one event. After the King had reviewed two regiments of French and Swiss guards on the plain of Sablons, Mehmed Efendi and his retinue had admired the equestrian maneuver of the ladies dressed as Amazons. The contemporary French accounts commented on how the eyes of all the Ottomans were uniquely attached to the ladies, as it was not customary to see Ottoman women in similar maneuvers. When in Constantinople, Bonnac and the Frenchmen who had brought Mehmed Efendi back were invited that same week by the Grand Vezir. Bonnac had just started describing the Amazons when the Grand Vezir smiled and interrupted to say that Mehmed Efendi had already talked to him about that.[23] He continued to explain that the Ottoman women had a very different education; they hardly left the harem, let alone joined the troops.

The Grand Vezir then mentioned the beauty of the French kingdom, the number of its inhabitants, and the royal canal of Languedoc which he called the site of marvels. Also, on another occasion,[24] when Bonnac wanted to review the capitulations with the Grand Vezir, İbrahim Paşa replied that "the ministers of the French Emperor conferred with Mehmed Efendi on that subject, and on his return, Mehmed Efendi had informed him of their claim." These indicated the amount of oral communication that must have taken place at least between Mehmed Efendi and the Grand Vezir İbrahim Paşa.

Mehmed Efendi had also gathered information in France about different European states. This information was effective in several policy decisions in the Ottoman Empire. The Venetian bailo reported in 1721[25] that Mehmed Efendi had returned from the West with the advice that "aid to the Pretender (James III) would be a good way of opposing Austria, and if he was restored, he would not fail to be well understood by Austria's enemies." In another report,[26] the bailo stated that, in relation to the Ottoman-Russian rivalry over

Persia, the Porte interpreted the Czar's going to St. Petersburg from Moscow according to Mehmed Efendi's suggestions. Mehmed Efendi, on his return from France, had given "a warning against wishful thinking by saying there was nothing more obscure in the world than the conduct of the Czar."

Contemporary French evidence external to the account is sufficient to reconstruct the oral report that Mehmed Efendi had presented to the Ottoman chain of command. One Ottoman political motive in dispatching this embassy was to seek cooperation with France and Spain against Austria. Mehmed Efendi presented this proposal to the French cabinet and was rejected.[27]

The other Ottoman political motive was to get France to put pressure on the Knights of Malta who were raiding Ottoman vessels. When Mehmed Efendi asked the Duc d'Orleans to stop the Knights of Malta, the Regent responded that he could not do anything without the consent of Malta.[28] The regent also had to consider the Pope's attitude since he protected the Knights of Malta. According to the Pope, the knights had to be supported in carrying on their perpetual crusade.[29] The Ottomans finally managed to stop the Malta knights by making the Christian merchants pay for the Maltese pillages. Christian powers were forced to have the grand master of Malta renounce the attacks against the Ottomans.[30]

The final political mission, which caused great friction, was to obtain the liberty of Ottoman slaves who were kept in the French galleys contrary to the agreements reached in various treaties.[31] The clashes of Mehmed Efendi with Dubois, the French foreign minister, appear in varying degrees in different transcriptions of the embassy account. Mehmed Efendi's long description of the matter was the only instance in his account where his anger penetrated through his solemn reporting. Bonnac had to delete the passages where Mehmed Efendi expressed his resentment against Dubois.[32] Mehmed Efendi had initially paid a ceremonial visit to Dubois on Bonnac's insistence.[33] Tension arose when Dubois did not return Mehmed Efendi's visit. When Mehmed Efendi asked the reason from the interpreter, he was told that Dubois was very busy so they should go visit him instead. Mehmed Efendi rejected the suggestion. A few days later the interpreter suggested they should not offend Dubois since he was preparing gifts for Mehmed Efendi—and this reasoning angered Mehmed Efendi even more.

After persistent inquiries, the interpreter admitted that Dubois had not come because he had claims on the post of prime ministry. Since prime ministers did not visit ambassadors, Dubois did not want to pay a visit either. This reply rightfully upset Mehmed Efendi; he asked why Dubois had then visited the Austrian, English, and Dutch ambassadors. If Dubois had pretensions about being the prime minister, he should at least learn how an Ottoman prime minister treated an ambassador, said Mehmed Efendi. He added that, according to Ottoman standards, there was not a single seigneur of the court except Villeroi who had invited him to eat with him; "for honors of speech, the French have been so generous as to be the most devoted people of the world— to that, the proverb 'eat our souls but do not touch our plates' can be applied."[34] In the end, Dubois came to pay a visit to Mehmed Efendi.

Mehmed Efendi, returning Dubois' visit, remarked in his account that he had seen Dubois three times. According to Mehmed Efendi, in all their conversations, Dubois "could not restrain himself from opening his mouth only to release another lie from his reservoir."[35] Mehmed Efendi had a list of the forty Ottoman slaves who had belonged to households of his friends in Constantinople and had been captured by the French. These slaves had been sent to the French galleys. Mehmed Efendi had asked for French assistance to locate these slaves and return them to him. Dubois said they had no information because of the plague. Then he claimed that, in any case, the slaves were not imprisoned but worked in transportation where they could collect their ransom money. Mehmed Efendi replied that he would be willing to provide the money if the French did not release them voluntarily.[36] Dubois retorted that the French King was not a slave merchant. The captains of the vessels had bought the slaves, not the King. Mehmed Efendi reasoned that since the vessels belonged to the King and their captains were appointed by the King, the slaves in the vessels belonged to the King, not to the captains. Mehmed Efendi's power in discourse came through this vehement argument. He successfully countered all the arguments presented by Dubois.

Dubois gave up and asked for another copy of the list of the slaves Mehmed Efendi wanted delivered.[37] Mehmed Efendi waited expectantly for these slaves until he embarked at Montpellier. When the slaves did not arrive, he left France and stated in his account that this had been just another lie of Dubois.[38] Yet the French did return the Ottoman slaves to Constantinople a few months later; the delay had been caused by Mehmed Efendi's list. The list only contained the forty names without further description. The French reviewed their slave registers. Corresponding to only the first person on Mehmed Efendi's list, a certain "Mehmed Ali," the French located a dozen slaves by the same name. They then asked Mehmed Efendi for additional descriptions of the persons listed to clarify the situation; Mehmed Efendi could not provide that information. In the end, the French freed eighty prisoners instead of forty.[39]

In Constantinople, all these disillusionments led Mehmed Efendi to treat the Frenchmen, especially Bonnac, who had arranged for his meeting with Dubois, with great coldness. One of the Frenchmen noted the extent of Mehmed Efendi's distance at the reception of the Grand Admiral; "Mehmed Efendi gave each of us civilities," he said, "but so cold and reserved, that we could not respond and were scandalized. . . . Grand Admiral was not comfortable so Marquis de Bonnac proposed to bring our musicians and some bottles of champagne to break down the coldness . . . but the proposition was not accepted since the presence of the religious scholars would have embarrassed the Grand Admiral.''[40] In another context, Mehmed Efendi dissuaded the Grand Vezir from giving a large feast for the Frenchmen.[41] He also told everyone that Bonnac was not at all on good terms with Dubois.

Yet some of this coldness of Mehmed Efendi was due to his personal clashes with Bonnac. On his return, when Bonnac heard how unfavorably Mehmed Efendi spoke of him, he decided to make him sorry.[42] The Grand Vezir had demanded a list from Mehmed Efendi of all the gifts Mehmed Efendi had been given. On this list, Mehmed Efendi did not report a number of the items he had received. The French dragomans came and described these concealed items to Bonnac. Bonnac sent to the Grand Vezir a nécessaire, similar to the one Mehmed Efendi had not reported, in the name of Madame Bonnac. This pleased the Grand Vezir. Yet the message delivered by the dragoman told the Grand Vezir that ''this (gift) was 'necessary' for a Grand Vezir, yet the one given to Mehmed Efendi in France was fit for a King.'' The Grand Vezir immediately sent for the necessaire Mehmed Efendi had kept for himself and likewise obliged Mehmed Efendi to surrender four carpets and subsequently some mirrors. This incident could also have caused Mehmed Efendi to take a stand against Bonnac and the other Frenchmen. In spite of this personal reaction to the Frenchmen, however, Mehmed Efendi continued to talk to all his friends about the beauties he saw in the French kingdom.[43]

Some of the things Mehmed Efendi excluded from his account, those traced through contemporary French accounts, must have been included in these talks. He must have mentioned the museum of M. d'Ozombrai[44] which contained a mass of curiosities related to all parts of physics, mathematics, and natural history. The assemblage of magnets, changing liquid colors, phosphores, and anatomies in wax had greatly impressed Mehmed Efendi. He had also visited the Sorbonne where the faculty received him in their ceremonial robes.[45] The faculty had initially wanted to receive him during the discussion of a religious thesis. The government did not deem fit for Mehmed Efendi to attend a dispute on the Christian religion, so he did not take part in the discussion.

Mehmed Efendi also intervened and requested from the King and Duc d'Orleans the punishment of an imposter Mustafa Ağa who was residing in Paris.[46] Mustafa Ağa had been a cook in Paris. He had then gone to Venice, acquired a false letter of kinship to Ahmed III, and had given himself the title of Ottoman prince. After fighting with the Venetian troops against the Ottomans, he had been given employment and a pension in the French army. The

French King, in order to please Mehmed Efendi, ordered Mustafa Ağa to leave Paris in twenty-four hours and retreat to Montbelliard. On his return to Constantinople, Mehmed Efendi must have informed the Sultan and the Grand Vezir about this action.

Mehmed Efendi's being an extraordinary ambassador with a very high status placed restrictions on his account; he did not mention the various French games he had encountered ranging from *biribi,* a game of chance, to *jeu de paume,* a sport. Saint Simon[47] described the night Mehmed Efendi was given a grand meal by Duc de Lauzun with *biribi.* Mehmed Efendi did not know what *biribi* was. He watched the game and wanted to play afterwards; he won two or three times and appeared delighted. Mehmed Efendi also did not mention the sword play he attended at a hall where he watched a hundred different assaults of the sword and admired them.[48] *Jeu de paume,* a particular racquet game, was another attraction he saw but did not note in his account.[49]

After writing his account, Mehmed Efendi settled down to his previous occupation. He held several accounting posts in Constantinople and was then sent to Egypt as a scribe. During the Patrona revolt in 1730, since he was one of Sultan Ahmed III's and the Grand Vezir's men, he was deported to the island of Cyprus and died there a year later.[50] His impact on the course of the Ottoman Empire revealed itself mostly through his son.

Mehmed Efendi's son, Mehmed Said, was approximately twenty-five years old when he joined his father on the embassy to Paris as his personal secretary.[51] The interaction with French society affected him more than his father. Mehmed Said's age and status during the embassy gave him more freedom to experiment with the French way of life. Mehmed Said was mentioned for the first time in the accounts of la Beaune[52] at Sète who described Said as "a man of calm character who tries to understand French . . . already knowing a few phrases, he pretends to understand a part of the conversation." There was a willingness on Mehmed Said's part to learn a different language and understand a different culture.

In Paris, he was occasionally entertained separately from his father. Since he did not have to observe protocol as closely as his father, he participated more in French society. He learned to sculpt in wood from Madame Maubois who was also the King's teacher.[53] One night, "chaperoned by Madame de Polignac and Madame d'O, Mehmed Said attended a feast given by the Prince de Conti . . . one thing was certain, the son of the ambassador and his physician were dead drunk at five in the morning."[54] This incident was followed by similar ones as Mehmed Said spent two days with a lady in the labyrinth at the park of Versailles and was very drunk.[55] Mehmed Said very easily adapted to the French way of life and was fluent in French by the time of his return. On the way back, attending a ball at Lyon,[56] he asked Madame

Portrait of Mehmed Said Efendi, son of Yirmisekiz Çelebi Mehmed Efendi. The painting was executed by Aved in Paris during Mehmed Said's embassy; it is located in Musée National du Château de Versailles. (*Cliché des Musées Nationaux*)

Poulletier to sing 'l'acte turc' of "L'Europe Galante"—a sign indicating both his access to and retention of French music. When the French ships taking Mehmed Efendi and his retinue back to Constantinople stopped in Tunisia, Said Efendi sent letters to Paris. He "wrote letters to his friends in Paris, in French and with his own hand, in a very polite manner."[57] Although these contemporary French accounts could have been overstating some events, those events still document Mehmed Said's participation in the activities of French society.

Mehmed Said's particular reaction to this cultural encounter foreshadowed the development of a new kind of Ottoman personality oriented toward the West and Western culture. This personality was soon going to help steer the Ottoman Empire toward Western waters.

4

The Impact of the Embassy

Yet the important fact was that there now was, even though limited to a small number of people, a tolerance in the attitude to the outside (the West). With this tolerance, the lives of foreigners in Istanbul also became more free; the mediating groups (Ottoman minorities) surrounding these foreigners slowly started to emulate Western manners. . . . In fact, a door (to the West) that had stayed closed until then was opening. In spite of various reactions, this course of events was to continue throughout the century.[1]

The impact of the embassy was different in French and Ottoman societies. The impact in France was temporary; it manifested itself as a fashion that gradually faded away. In the Ottoman Empire, the impact was permanent. The embassy heralded the beginning of many ensuing changes in Ottoman society.

The fashion that escalated in France as a consequence of this embassy was the Turquerie, the imitation of a Turkish taste in attire and decoration. Turquerie was part of a larger trend that had emerged during the reign of Louis XIV and his successors. During this period, "the preromantic vogue of Orientalism and the cult of Chinoiserie permeated the art, literature, and philosophy of the age. Gardens were altered in the Oriental fashion; Chinese pottery, furniture, lacquer painting were reproduced. . . . Tapestries, embroideries, designs for dresses were influenced by the Chinese design. . . . To have a monkey or a green parrot was a sign of luxurious refinement."[2] This development paralleled the increasing European commercial interest and presence in the Orient.

A previous Ottoman mission to France in 1669 during the reign of Louis XIV[3] had affected French literature. The manners of the Ottoman envoy had fascinated Louis XIV who asked Molière to include a Turkish episode in his play *Le Bourgeois Gentilhomme*. Some efforts were made to achieve authenticity in its presentation as the French envoy to the Porte, d'Arvieux, did the costuming. Molière himself included a few phrases of Turkish in addition to

72

some gibberish and lingua franca. Lully added some pseudo-exotic music with the tambourine. This scene set the model for many to follow; Turkish scenes continued to be inserted in French plays for popularity and pleasure. Turkish interludes were also inserted in ballets.

The most intriguing aspect of Ottoman life involved the Palace and the harem.[4] Many operas, plays, and popular novels based on the lives of various Sultans started to be written in the West. Some examples of the operas, for example, are *Tamerlane* based on the conflict between Bayezid II and Timur, by Handel (1724), *Muhammed II* (rule 1451–1481) by Reinhard Keiser (1693), and *Solimano* (Süleyman I, rule 1520–1566) first by Hasse (1753) then by Perez (1757). The West was incorporating some Ottoman topics into their culture unlike the Ottomans who continued to be culturally closed to the West.

The Ottoman topics used by the Europeans ignored the precise details of Ottoman life, however. The characters spoke and acted like Europeans. More realistic interpretations came only later in the second half of the eighteenth century starting with the *Libretto of Soliman II ou Les Trois Sultanes* by Charles-Simon Favart in 1761.[5] This libretto was based on rivalry among the female slaves of the Harem. The role of Roxelane was performed by Madame Favart who wore, for the first time in performing arts, an authentic Ottoman costume specially ordered from Constantinople.[6] This play became very popular and was performed in many courts of Europe. Such cultural interaction between the courts of Europe helped diffuse the Ottoman impact. One widespread influence of the Ottomans in the West was the military music of the Janissary band[7] which accompanied Turks in their battles. The first ruler to receive such a military band was Augustus II (rule 1697–1704) of Poland; he was quickly followed by Russia, Austria, France, and other states. By 1770, most European armies had similar bands.

The impact of Mehmed Efendi's embassy occurred within this framework. A whole series of engravings and paintings were produced in Paris depicting the ambassador at the different places visited.[8] M. Coypel prepared a painting of the audience of Mehmed Efendi with the King. This painting was going to be used to make a Gobelin tapestry. M. Coypel presented a sketch of this painting to the King.[9] Painter P. D. Martin pictured Mehmed Efendi on the Malaquais quay returning from his audience with the King. A tapestry realized at Gobelin in the atelier of Lefebvre had been inspired by a painting of C. Parrocel; it depicted the entrance of Mehmed Efendi to the Tuileries. Mehmed Efendi also gave permission to Sieur Justinar to make his portrait.[10] These were the only indications of the impact of the Ottoman embassy on the French.

All these impacts were temporary; the French treated the Ottoman embassy

MME. FAVART Role de Roxelane.

Pensionnaire du Roi, recue a la Comédie Italienne en 1752.

Actress Madame Favart in her Ottoman costume. She had the costume especially brought from Constantinople for her role in the play *Les Trois Sultanes*. (*Phot. Bibl. Nat., Paris*) merely as a source for a new fashion and briefly reflected its effect either in their attire or in their paintings. The French impact on Ottoman society was permanent. Aesthetically, a new taste started to emerge as the Ottomans began imitating French architecture, garden construction, and design. Technologically, the printing press, introduced through the efforts of Mehmed Said Efendi, became a permanent component of Ottoman society.

The French impact on Ottoman society was felt most during the Tulip Era. This era was marked by intense construction activity, especially within Constantinople. In 1719, İbrahim Paşa built the Çırağan Palace in Beşiktaş, a complex of school, library, fountain, and a mausoleum near Şehzade mosque in 1720, two new summer palaces in 1720 and 1724, and the Şerefabad palace along the Bosphorus in Üsküdar in 1728. He also built many fountains throughout Istanbul.[11] In 1726, he presented a palace and a summer residence to Sultan Ahmed III; the palace, Neşatabad, was on the Bosphorus, and the summer residence was in Topkapı Palace.[12]

The Sultan himself also constructed a library in the Topkapı Palace in 1719, a palace, Emnabad, along the Bosphorus in Fındıklı for his daughter Fatma sultan in 1725, and a fountain in front of the Topkapı Palace in 1729.[13] The active participation of the Sultan in these constructions was evident in his correspondence with İbrahim Paşa. He wrote: "Today I went to the waterside residence that was being repaired. . . . All was ordered; it is proceeding well. My daughter's waterside residence needs some repair. I showed it to the ağa; he will go tomorrow and purchase all that is needed."[14]

The intense construction activity during the Tulip Era was epitomized in the construction of the Sa'dabad (the site containing palaces, gardens, and canals at Sweet Waters of Europe in Constantinople) complex.[15] Its construction was also indicative of the French influence in architecture. The whole construction tried to imitate Versailles and Fontainebleau, which Mehmed Efendi had visited. Mehmed Efendi brought back plans of these palaces to apply them in Constantinople.

Recently, a series of twelve engravings have been disclosed in the Topkapı Museum Library. These engravings, dating from 1714, depict various sites at Versailles.[16] There are short descriptions of the sites in Ottoman at the top of each engraving. These descriptions contain more information about the sites than that provided by the French subtitles. In one engraving, the Ottoman description states that the water jets of the Fountain de Latone look "like silver belts."[17] In another fountain, the water jets "take the shape of a silver cypress grove."[18] These descriptions suggest that the Ottoman titles were written by someone who had visited these sites. Mehmed Efendi was the most recent Ottoman ambassador to visit Paris after 1714, when these engravings

Engraving of the view of the Versailles palace from the orange orchard, which can be found in the Topkapı Museum Library. This was probably among the engravings Mehmed Efendi brought back from France. The engravings have annotations in Ottoman; this one is translated as "this is the view of the Versailles palace from in front of the pool which is next to the bitter orange orchard." The fact that the information is more detailed in Ottoman than in French suggests that the Ottoman translation was made by someone who had seen the Versailles firsthand. The engraving is located in the Topkapı Museum Library, Catalogue No. H1974. (*Courtesy of the Topkapı Museum Library, Istanbul*)

were drawn, and they were most probably brought back to Constantinople by him.

These engravings must have served as visual aids in the construction of Sa'dabad. The canal, copied most likely from Versailles, formed the most dominant feature of this new site. Before the foundation of the Sultan's summer palace, the river bed was widened into a canal with a marble quay constructed on both sides. The summer palace was then placed on thirty marble columns with a large pool in front; "waters poured into the pool through troughs which were designed like ornamental fountains."[19] Mehmed Efendi also gave the idea of extending the canal and planting trees on its course.[20] The expansive park was planned on the model of Versailles.[21]

Mehmed Efendi tried to replicate the architecture he saw in Paris. After his return to Constantinople, in a letter[22] to Villeroi he stated that "they [the Ottomans] were also expecting that he [Villeroi] send the printed plans of the royal houses and gardens which were promised to him. A number of architects were summoned from Europe to construct buildings in different styles."[23]

Employment of detailed plans in construction of houses for aesthetic reasons was a new concept. Ottoman architecture had tended to follow a random design; wings used to be added in any style whenever the need arose without taking into consideration the location of other houses. A different concept of proportion and symmetry was being introduced into Ottoman architecture; construction was now organized entirely in accordance with the plans supplied by the French.

The Sa'dabad construction started in June 1722. Under the personal surveillance of the Grand Vezir, the construction continued even on Mondays and Thursdays, which were state holidays.[24] The construction ended in August 1722; it had only taken sixty days to build. The supply of marble was one reason for the speed of the construction. The necessary marble did not come from the quarries. Instead, the ancient "tower of dogs" in Çengelköy on the Asiatic shore provided the blocks of fine marble for the wall along the canal and for the columns sustaining a portion of the roof of the palace.[25] The water in the canal flowed through two dykes, formed small waterfalls, and collected in a large marble pool. There were two balconies with glistening domes on either side. Within the pool, water jetted out of a dragon's mouth—similar to the pools Mehmed Efendi had seen in France. All along the canal, the Ottoman dignitaries were asked to build residences and places of retreat with vineyards and orchards in their gardens. This led to the construction of numerous residences and gardens around the site.[26] On its completion, İbrahim Paşa himself composed a couplet to celebrate the occasion which ran as "let it be blessed to Sultan Ahmed, to have eternal happiness in the state," thereupon naming the site *sa'dabad*, eternal happiness.[27] All the buildings on the site were similarly endowed with poetic names such as *hürremabad*, eternal joy, or *hayrabad*, eternal goodness. These names reflected the Persian influence current in Ottoman literature and arts during the Tulip Era.

Many eighteenth-century engravings and descriptions of the site exist. The engravings portrayed the new sense of symmetry in design and organization in construction.[28] Trees were all planted in one row. The water, running through steps, extended to the Sultan's palace. There was also a very vivid description of a visit to Sa'dabad by a Frenchman.[29] This Frenchman visited the site in the retinue of the French ambassador and his wife "who went to stroll in Sa'dabad accompanied by most of the French residents in Constantinople."[30]

Engraving of Sa'dabad in Constantinople. The drawing is in the book *Beauties of the Bosphorus* (London, 1840) by N. H. Bartlett; its model was a drawing by Miss Pardoe. The engraving is located in the Topkapı Museum Library, Catalogue No. YB1965. (*Courtesy of the Topkapı Museum Library, Istanbul*)

The description started by stating that the French influence in the construction of the site was very visible. According to the author, this influence was brought by "Mehmed Efendi who, upon his return, gave a detailed account of all the royal residences in the environs of Paris. His narration and the peace established by the Passarowitz treaty enabled the execution of a site similar in design to those sites in France."[31] After a detailed description of the canal, the Sultan's residence, and the gardens around the site, the Frenchman included information on the residences of the Ottoman dignitaries. There were presumably more than two hundred such residences, all built in different colors.[32] The Ottoman dignitaries identified their residences by hanging symbols describing their official duties on their doors. The residence of the supervisor of the dockyards had a small galley mounted on its door. The master-general of artillery set his residence apart by placing a wooden cannon painted in bronze on his door. Officers of the falconry had birds carved out of wood on their doors.

After this interesting observation on the residences, the Frenchman concluded his description. He referred to how the site of Sa'dabad had started to change Ottoman entertainment habits.

> It seems that the Turks have [attained] a change of spirit and inclination with the [establishment] of this place of pleasure. You know, Monsieur, that they have never been a people [fond] of promenade, they have become so. There are days when this place is frequented as much as the Cour la Reine and Champs Elisees (sic). People of the country and foreigners of all ages and sexes go there [to Sa'dabad] alone.[33]

This change was initiated by the change introduced in the use of space. Along with the French palace plans, a different use of space was introduced to Ottoman society.

Additional plans of palaces were brought from Paris by Monsieur Lenoir, the French translator at the French embassy in Constantinople.[34] Lenoir was sent to Paris by the Porte in 1722 to renew the proposition Mehmed Efendi had initially made without success about the alliance with France and Spain against Austria. This political motive of the voyage was disguised by the official statement that Lenoir "was sent to purchase a list of orders of the Grand Vezir."[35] The list of orders revealed the excitement with which the palace circles had received the gifts Mehmed Efendi had brought. Lenoir was ordered to bring a large variety of items.[36] Glasses for spectacles, watches, telescopes, microscopes, mirrors, and an anatomical head of wax represented the orders for technological products. These items could not be attained or produced in the Ottoman Empire since they were the products of a certain technological evolution. This newly emerging pattern of importing technological products without attempting to produce them in the Ottoman Empire was the first indication of a long history of technological dependency.

The rest of the orders were solely consumption items. Cotton cloth, tafettas, and other cloths were ordered for decoration; nécessaires, commodes, Gobelin carpets "without figures" were ordered to decorate, most probably the newly built Sa'dabad complex. Red, yellow, and white parrots, and hyacinths, anemones, jonquils, and buttercups were presumably ordered for the gardens and menageries of Sa'dabad. The final and most interesting item ordered for consumption was wine: a thousand bottles of champagne and five hundred,[37] or nine hundred,[38] bottles of Burgundy. This last item certainly deviated from the Ottoman mode of public life.

The gifts Mehmed Efendi had brought to Constantinople had been instrumental in initiating the Western impact; some items were ordered to be "more beautiful than those brought by Mehmed Efendi."[39] All these items were symbols associated with a certain mode of life that the Ottomans now wanted to imitate. Although the list was given by the Grand Vezir, the orders probably included the demands of the Palace circles. The French impact penetrated Ottoman society as French consumption patterns were emulated and promoted by the highest officials of the Ottoman Empire.

The Ottomans had, throughout their history, imitated various products of the societies they had come into contact with. As a dynamic expanding state, the Ottomans had the power to control and mold these impacts as they wanted. The Ottoman encounter with the French during the eighteenth century was initiated when the Ottomans had started to retreat militarily and technologically. The Ottomans were not strong enough to control and mold these impacts and the impacts started to mold the Ottomans into a new synthesis. This synthesis produced a new mode of life and a new personality type in the Ottoman Empire.

The new personality, the leading Ottoman elite of the future, was exemplified by Mehmed Said Efendi, son of Yirmisekiz Çelebi Mehmed Efendi. He was the first Ottoman statesman to learn and speak French—or indeed any Western language.[40] Mehmed Said had oriented himself toward the West. On his return to Constantinople, he held various important secretarial positions.

In 1741, Mehmed Said Efendi was appointed as the Ottoman ambassador to Paris.[41] During his six-month residence in Paris, Mehmed Said distinguished himself by his mastery of the French language, customs, and manners. He was particularly fond of the operas and plays of the Comédie Française.[42] At the many balls he attended, he openly drank wine. Mehmed Said also had his picture painted by the academician M. Aved. In the portrait, "Mehmed Said was surrounded by items revealing some information about him like the sphere, the map, peace treaty, and an atlas, the first book to be printed under his sponsorship in Constantinople."[43] Twenty years between the embassies of the father and the son revealed great change. Mehmed Said Efendi was able to participate with great ease and enjoy the entertainments his father had encountered for the first time.

After his return from Paris, Mehmed Said Efendi held various posts. He became the Grand Vezir in 1755. He was dismissed from office after five months. As a reason for his dismissal, one source cites his attempts to impose new taxes and his "predisposition to adapt to the currents of change in his times."[44] After holding governorships in various cities, he died while he was the governor of Maraş.

The most important contribution of Mehmed Said Efendi to the Ottoman Empire was his establishment of the Ottoman printing press with the assistance of İbrahim Müteferrika.[45] This seems to have been the singular most important technological consequence of Mehmed Efendi's embassy to Paris. On his return, Mehmed Said Efendi founded the printing press around 1726 with Müteferrika, a Hungarian convert to Islam. The introduction of printing was technologically possible because of the presence of Jewish, Greek, and Armenian printers in Constantinople who had been printing books in Hebrew, Greek, and Armenian.[46] Because the equipment and skilled personnel were already there, the Ottoman printing press could be successfully established. Contemporary historians explained the delay in the establishment of an Ottoman printing press by Ottoman religious conservatism and the large number of calligraphers the state wanted to keep employed.[47] Once the printing press was established, however, it maintained itself even after the Patrona revolt which ended the Tulip Era in 1730.[48]

Mehmed Said and İbrahim Müteferrika stated that they wanted to establish the printing press to advance science and promulgate education in the Ottoman Empire. The printing press would supply books for the students, correct the mistakes of calligraphers, and preserve the manuscripts that were demolished and destroyed by fires and revolutions.[49] These two men attempted to identify a problem and solve it through a Western innovation.

All the other French technological products were too advanced to be produced in the Ottoman Empire. The Ottoman technological level limited the receptivity of Ottoman society. That society could not produce advanced technological products, but could consume them through continuous imports. Ottoman society was most receptive toward luxury goods. As the customs associated with these goods also penetrated into the Ottoman way of life, cultural transformation commenced. Divisions in Ottoman society sharpened as some Ottomans became oriented toward the West while others rejected it.

The Ottoman interaction with the West through the embassy of Mehmed Efendi in 1721 created enduring impacts on Ottoman society. A new taste and way of life was created as Ottomans emulated French cultural products; customs and ideas associated with these products gradually entered Ottoman society and created a cultural dichotomy among the Ottomans. A new type of Ottoman emerged, oriented toward the West and assimilating Western culture. Finally, the Ottoman printing press was established for the first time, enabling the spread of information and knowledge to a larger number of people. These people who now gained access to knowledge through a technological innovation sustained the Western impact within the Ottoman administration. The conservative-progressive tension that gradually eroded the Empire at the very end was established.

II

Factors Affecting the Interaction and the Western Impact

5

Comparison of
Three Ottoman Embassies

The embassy of Yirmisekiz Çelebi Mehmed Efendi to Paris in the years 1720–1721 reflected an increasing Ottoman receptivity to the West, which can be historically documented.

The historical value of the information provided by the embassy account of Yirmisekiz Çelebi Mehmed Efendi can only be assessed through comparisons with other Ottoman embassies. These comparisons reveal several factors that affect the information provided by an embassy. These factors are the medium, the historical context, the stimuli in either society to initiate such an embassy and the motives behind it, the barriers, and the characteristics of the persons appointed as ambassadors. The specific nature of Mehmed Efendi's embassy emerges from this comparative evaluation.

The embassy of Yirmisekiz Çelebi Mehmed Efendi to Paris in 1720–1721 can be compared with the embassy of Kara Mehmed Paşa to Vienna in 1665 and the embassy of Yirmisekiz Çelebizade Mehmed Said Efendi to Stockholm in 1732–1733. Kara Mehmed Paşa's embassy account is the first printed account of an Ottoman embassy to a European state before Mehmed Efendi.[1] The embassy of Mehmed Said Efendi is the first printed account of an Ottoman embassy to a European state after Mehmed Efendi. Mehmed Said Efendi was also Mehmed Efendi's son; the differences in their accounts might reveal the changing Ottoman orientation toward the West.

Medium

An embassy as a medium is different from other possible media of communication between societies. These other media consist of wars conducted by soldiers, commercial exchanges by merchants, forced transfers of slaves, religious travels by pilgrims, professional travels by artisans seeking work, and students going for education. All these different patterns of interaction focus on different aspects of a society; artisans and merchants are concerned with economic activities, missionaries and pilgrims focus on religious institutions, students are involved with educational institutions. Tradesmen represent trade companies and missionaries represent certain religious sects. None of these groups claim to represent their societies in their dealings except soldiers and ambassadors. During wars, societies seek to minimize all interactions with each other. Embassies are the only peaceful medium in wartime between societies where the societies are willing to communicate.

Historical Context

The Ottomans fought three wars at the beginning of the eighteenth century. They were defeated in a war against Austria, Poland, Venice, and Russia which concluded with the Carlowitz treaty in 1699. The Ottomans defeated the Russians in a war that ended with the Pruth peace in 1711. Their third war was against Venice and Austria. It ended with an Ottoman defeat and concluded with the Passarowitz treaty in 1718. These wars revealed the Russians and the Austrians as the two important adversaries of the Ottomans, who tried to form alliances countering them. Among the Western powers on the continent, France was the only formidable power with the same adversaries. France had also maintained long satisfactory diplomatic relations with the Ottoman Empire; there had not been any direct military clashes between France and the Ottoman Empire. In addition, the French had good trade relations with the Ottomans. The Ottoman attitude toward France was therefore favorable and receptive.

The embassy of Kara Mehmed Paşa to Vienna took place to fulfill the clause of the Vasvar treaty requiring an embassy exchange between the Ottoman and Austrian Empires.[2] The Ottoman campaign against Austria started in 1663 and the Ottomans captured many Austrian castles. When the Austrians were defeated in their retaliation during the spring of 1664, they sued for peace. The Ottomans still regarded the Austrians as enemies with whom they had had many conflicts and viewed them, unlike the French, with suspicion and sometimes hostility.

The historical context of Mehmed Said Efendi's embassy to Stockholm in 1732–1733 was different from either of the other embassies. Ottoman relations with Sweden had started to strengthen when the Swedish King Charles XII fought with an Ottoman opponent, the Russians, in 1707.[3] King Charles was defeated at Poltava in 1709 and had to take refuge in the Ottoman Empire. He stayed in the Ottoman Empire for five years. On his departure, he borrowed two thousand purses of money from the Ottoman treasury. After reaching Sweden, he was killed during a war with Denmark in 1718; his debt was not paid by the Swedes. Grand Vezir İbrahim Paşa, reviewing the financial situation of the Ottoman Empire, decided to send an envoy, Kozbekçi Mustafa Ağa, to collect the loan.[4] Sweden, claiming an economic crisis, asked for a postponement and was granted one until Mehmed Said's embassy. The Ottoman relations with Sweden were neither adversarial nor friendly. The Swedes were distant from the Ottoman Empire and had the promise of being allies against Russia. The Ottomans had not had many associations with the Swedes as they had with the French and Austrians. The Ottoman attitude toward Sweden was indeterminate. Among the three embassies, the Ottoman embassy to Paris was the most conducive to Ottoman receptivity toward the West.

Stimulus

Ottoman military defeats had provided the stimulus for the Ottoman embassy to Paris in 1720–1721. The embassy to Vienna in 1665 was initiated as a requirement of the Vasvar peace treaty; this effort was viewed as a way to foster friendly relations between the two states. Different factors led to Mehmed Said Efendi's embassy to Stockholm in 1732–1733. Ottoman loans to Sweden were a topic of joint concern. The actual stimulus, however, was generated by an Ottoman need to assess Sweden's international position. The Ottomans wanted to evaluate Sweden's relationship with Russia.

These different stimuli shaped the attitude of the embassies. The embassy to Paris was inquisitive and instructional, the embassy to Vienna was procedural, whereas the embassy to Stockholm was observational. The embassy to Paris was again the most positive.

Aim

The embassy to Paris had several aims; the one that appeared for the first time ever for an Ottoman embassy was "to visit fortresses and factories, and to make a thorough study of means of civilization and education, and report on those suitable for application in the Ottoman Empire."[5] This represented an Ottoman effort to catch up with the West. The extensive description by Kara Mehmed Paşa of the fortifications of the castle of Vienna[6] in his brief embassy report, pointed to a military concern. Evliya Çelebi,[7] whose reports supplement the Paşa's, also gave ample information on the fortifications all along the way to and in the castle of Vienna. The hope of future combats provided a military aim for the Ottoman embassy. The information gathered by this embassy must have been useful in the Ottoman siege of Vienna in 1683.

A letter attached to the manuscript of the embassy account directly revealed the secret aim for the embassy to Stockholm.[8] This letter, sent to the Sultan by the Grand Vezir, also exemplifies a source of information that did not exist for the other two embassy accounts:

> The contents of the imperial decree issued for the Swedish matter has been known to this humble servant. The Imperial consideration on the essence of the matter is excellent. The weak condition of the Swede and its alliance and dependence on the Muscovite had been previously heard by this humble servant. Then, since there had been no such [Imperial] consideration, not much time was allocated to investigate and examine the matter. This time, in accordance with the issued Imperial order [we will] investigate and obtain information from experts on whether an alliance between the Swede and the Muscovite, and the dependence of the Swede on the Muscovite exists or not. [And] after submitting the report to the royal presence, if necessary, discussion will begin with the Swedish ambassador. As the amount of the Swedish debt to the Porte was formerly noted by the Finance Department on the margin, it being evident from the margin that their debt is two hundred fifty thousand *guruş,* the paper [with the note] in the margin has been presented to the threshold of the exalted sovereign.

It was clear that the Ottomans, in order to shape their own policy, tried to assess Sweden's position in relation to Russia; this was the prevalent aim of the embassy.

The embassy to Vienna was aimed at and limited to an assessment of Austrian military strength. In the Swedish case, the Ottomans tried to assess the Swedish-Russian relationship in order to formulate an international policy decision. The embassy to Paris was the only embassy where the Ottomans were genuinely interested in French society in and of itself.

Barriers

The barriers between the Ottoman Empire and the West were similar for all Ottoman embassies: language, religion, food, and eating and entertaining habits. The quarantine obstacle Mehmed Efendi encountered on his voyage to Paris did not exist for Kara Mehmed Paşa or Mehmed Said Efendi. The Austrians and Swedes did not have quarantines at the time. The language problem was resolved by translators. Differences in food, eating, and entertainment were bravely tolerated by Mehmed Efendi.

Kara Mehmed Paşa was not interested in Austrian society enough to even recognize the barriers. His account revolved around descriptions of diplomatic procedures. The language barrier was overcome through translators.[9] Rather than participating in Austrian life, the Paşa preferred to entertain with his retinue. Evliya Çelebi narrated how the Paşa, on one occasion, disregarded the Austrian invitation and kept playing jereed with his soldiers for entertainment.[10] Although the Paşa stayed in Vienna for nine months, he did not give any information about the Austrian religion, food, or eating and entertainment habits except on two occasions. He once related the extreme respect and attention he was shown at a feast in the King's mother's garden.[11] Evliya Çelebi, who accompanied Kara Mehmed Paşa, described this feast in great detail.[12] The site had many vineyards, fruit orchards, and palaces where entertainment consisted of strange depictions of dragons in strange shapes, of pools flooding the ground, and of men imitating animals. On the other occasion, the Paşa referred to the food allocations he and his retinue were given. He stated that the Austrians had allocated previous ambassadors enough provision for one hundred twenty people.[13] Since Mehmed Paşa's retinue consisted of two hundred ninety-five, the Austrians increased the provisions.[14]

The embassy account of Mehmed Said Efendi is more informative about the barriers to communication. The language barrier was reduced in the case of Mehmed Said who knew French. Mehmed Said was also very observant of Swedish society and gave long descriptions on various aspects of his embassy as his father had done ten years ago in Paris. He described how enthusiastically he had been received by the Swedes.[15]

They were as happy as a Moor who had found goods. . . . [To watch our arrival] they filled up all the space in houses, shops, rooftops, and in addition, all the ships and even the ropes tying the ships to the port where [on] every rope [they] looked like a bunch of grapes. . . . The people, upon seeing us, waved their hats in the air and altogether cried in their own tongue, "long live the Padişah of the Ottomans."

This vivid description of the reception was followed by an event that revealed the difference in eating habits. Mehmed Said related how Swedes tried to take into account the Islamic eating habits which were different from theirs. He stated:

For dinner, the King sent a well equipped meal prepared on his own dining set. In addition, he had said "we know the people of Islam do not eat our meals but we took great care in preparing this meal by making special new courses." This slave . . . consumed a few candied fruit and coffee.[16]

There was an effort on Mehmed Said's side to accommodate Swedish preparations by accepting their meal, yet only consuming the things he judged proper by Islamic standards. He too bravely tolerated the differences in consumption habits like his father.

Mehmed Efendi was very observant of Swedish mannerisms as well. He noted how Swedes accentuated their conversations with gestures. "The King came toward this slave," he said, "and grabbed me by the hand inquiring over and over about my health."[17] On his last visit to the King, the King gave his personal word of honor to Mehmed Said for the payment of the Swedish debt, and "squeezed Mehmed Said's back with his hand."[18]

Mehmed Said Efendi also provided detailed descriptions on various aspects of Swedish society:[19] their physique ("strong, tall, with handsome faces, where many eighty year olds are in still good condition"), the port of Stockholm ("like the Istanbul port"), the city ("with straight paved streets, where the houses are not like those in Europe"),[20] the inhabitants ("who are friendly and enjoy showing courtesy to strangers"), the produce ("fruit is very scarce, especially grapes and pomegranate cannot be found at all; there are men who have not seen fresh grapes and pomegranate; I even promised to send sweet melon and watermelon seeds to the King who requested them"), the rites of the land ("there is not a jobless man left in their provinces—they have found jobs even for the poor; most of the vendors at the shops are women; their soldiers are prepared, clean and heroic"), and their orientation ("the populace of Sweden all including young and old, women and children, are enemies of the Muscovites to such a degree that if a person praises the Muscovites, that very minute they become enemies of that person").[21]

In addition to being accommodating to Swedish manners, Mehmed Said was able to transcend all barriers to provide a full description of Swedish life. The barriers decreased in importance as Ottoman interest in the West increased.

Agents

The specific characteristics of the three ambassadors had important effects on the embassies. Yirmisekiz Çelebi Mehmed Efendi and his son Mehmed Said Efendi were Ottoman educated gentlemen (çelebi). They were literate, had been educated in the religious sciences, literature, and poetry, and held important administrative posts. Mehmed Said Efendi was the clerk of the cavalry corps (sipahiler katibi); he was also an assistant to the chief secretary of the Grand Vezir (mektubı-i sadrazamı kalemi hülefasından). Kara Mehmed Paşa, however, was a soldier, the head of the Palace Guards (bostancı odabaşı). These differences in background affected their communication with Western societies. Mehmed Efendi and Mehmed Said Efendi were inquisitive, observant, and accommodating. Kara Mehmed Paşa was suspicious and rather hostile.

The Grand Vezir Fazıl Ahmed Paşa had been aware of Kara Mehmed Paşa's limitations as a soldier-diplomat. The Vezir made sure that learned men accompanied the Paşa on his embassy. According to Evliya Çelebi's account,[22] the Grand Vezir said to Kara Mehmed:

> Look, paşa! Are you going to go to the King as an ambassador in this outfit? Quickly put your men and your household together in a perfect manner. . . . Take well-informed men from among soldiers and tradesmen with you. You were trained and brought up in the corps of the Palace Guards. You do not know the circumstances of the Austrian frontier. We still have with us a world-traveler, a companion of mankind called Evliya. . . . He knows the conditions of frontiers, take him with you.

Although Evliya could have been exaggerating matters to increase his own importance, the consideration by the Grand Vezir still indicates the importance placed on the qualities of the ambassadors.

The background of Kara Mehmed Paşa as a soldier affected his perception of the Austrians. He viewed each meeting with the Austrians as a new combat that had to be won without giving any ground. The conflict over the Ottoman entrance to the city of Vienna exemplified this attitude.[23] The Austrians asked the Ottomans to lower their banners and standards and to stop playing their drums and kettledrums in their entrance to the city of Vienna. This had been the custom followed by all the former ambassadors who had visited the city. The Paşa insisted on marching as he had intended. Evliya Çelebi recounted the meetings Paşa had with the Austrians.[24] The Paşa declared the Austrian customs as "irreligious falsehoods of the infidels; he would do what the customs of Islam dictated, and march in." When the Austrians insisted, the Paşa threatened to notify the Grand Vezir not to disperse the Ottoman army (and to get ready instead to attack the Austrians for their misbehavior toward him). The Paşa proudly stated in his account that the Austrians gave in and let him march into the city.

The comparison of Kara Mehmed Paşa with Mehmed Efendi and Mehmed Said Efendi reveals the difference in orientation between the Ottoman "men of the sword" and "men of the pen."[25] Men of the sword were closed, combative, and challenging to the West while men of the pen were open, flexible, and accommodating. Even the accounts of Evliya Çelebi, himself a learned man, contrast sharply with the Paşa's embassy accounts of Vienna. Evliya Çelebi takes fifty pages to discuss his stay in Vienna,[26] telling about the former Ottoman siege of the city in 1528 by Süleyman the Magnificent, describing the castle and the numerous houses and palaces with vineyards and orchards, the marketplace with amazing craftsmen who excel in mechanical arts, churches, the inns and public baths, fountains, and various statues throughout the city. He then recounts a number of surgical operations he witnessed with great wonder and notes that he told the Paşa and his retinue about these experiences which impressed them as well. More information on the weather, the populace, the position of women, and agriculture all point to a person who was very observant of a foreign society. The Paşa's account does not contain any information on Austrian society except the negotiations over ceremonial procedures.

The similarity in the outlook of Evliya Çelebi to Mehmed Efendi and Mehmed Said Efendi suggests a common trait among the Ottoman learned "men of the pen." Both Mehmed Efendi's and his son's accounts are filled with information on the foreign culture; the populace, their manners, and patterns of life are all observed and noted in detail. These accounts exhibit a sense of curiosity as Mehmed Efendi and Mehmed Said Efendi sought knowledge on these foreign societies. In addition, the meetings with the French and Swedish, which were quite taxing at times, were handled with diplomatic finesse by relying on discourse rather than threat of war.

Mehmed Said Efendi, for example, recounted an incident with the King during a dinner.[27] The King, noting that the Ottomans were fighting the Persians, asked Said Efendi what the Sultan would do if the King were to go to the Sultan's assistance with twenty or thirty thousand soldiers. Said Efendi very carefully stated that the Sultan would be very delighted and would show the King extreme honor and courtesy. Yet, he said, "it is known to you that the Ottoman state has not needed anyone's help in its wars; whatever our conquests and victories, they occur by our own swords. You, our friends, do not need to trouble yourselves materially and physically. It is sufficient for you to help us here in spirit." This fine reply contrasts sharply with what Kara Mehmed Paşa's reaction might have been—an angry retort, at least.

The agents who carried out the embassies were important in structuring and affecting the Ottoman perception of the West. There was a noticeable difference between soldiers and scholars in their perceptions of foreign societies. Soldiers focused on comparisons of relative military strength. Scholars were more observant and receptive to the foreign societies; their mediations were more likely to affect and transform Ottoman perceptions of the West.

The accounts of the Ottoman embassies to Vienna and Stockholm supplement our information on the structure of Ottoman embassies. Evliya Çelebi gives information on how an Ottoman ambassador formed his retinue.[28] Kara Mehmed Paşa purchased, for three hundred seventy purses, the tools, weapons, ammunition, gold, and silver goods of the late Kıbleli Ali Paşa, İsmail Paşa, Ağa of the Jannissaries Salih Ağa, Serdar Ali Paşa, Can Arslan Paşa, Çatra Patra İsmail Paşa, and some other governors. All these Ottoman dignitaries had died in combat. Some of the men in the retinues of these deceased dignitaries must have also joined the retinue of Kara Mehmed Paşa. The additional men in the retinues came from gifts: Evliya notes the occasions where he was given, in addition to money and horses, a number of slaves as gifts by a provincial Paşa (of Eğri) on one occasion,[29] and by the Christian governor of the Semendire castle on another.[30] Evliya Çelebi and Kara Mehmed Paşa also searched throughout the embassy for some of their former men who were taken as captives in the preceding war with the Austrians. They were not successful in recovering them.

The embassy account of Mehmed Said Efendi also contains ample information on the hardships of the voyages. Since Mehmed Said Efendi was going to Sweden during the winter, weather presented substantial problems. Traveling mostly by sleighs, some of the people accompanying him—several were outside of his retinue—died from the severe cold; these included a Tatar and a *dhimmi* (non-Muslim Ottoman). The following day, a Tatar who was severely frostbitten killed his horse to warm himself up, but both died instantly. "By the assistance of Allah," Mehmed Said Efendi said, "none of us suffered any damage except one whose ear was hurt but cured later by medicine."[31]

The boat trip through the Baltic Sea toward Stockholm presented another challenge as the weather kept changing the direction of sail. The Baltic Sea was a very cold sea with severe storms, where

> the sails froze overnight in the position they had been left in and no-one could move them in another direction [until] around noontime the following day; again it was observed that ice as large as cushions froze on the ropes and reels, so that the sailors, using large axes, had to cut the ice with difficulty in a couple of hours and throw it into the sea.[32]

The final touch in the extremity of the weather was when it snowed on the eleventh day of June; "although they kept saying summer comes," an astonished Mehmed Said wrote, "this slave stayed there until the end of July; we did not see a single day that deserved to be called a summer day during our stay. Only exalted Allah knows if summer came after we left."[33]

Two interesting incidents in Mehmed Said's embassy account are not present in the other embassy accounts. These incidents reflect the wide spectrum of information the Ottoman ambassadors gathered during their embassies. One incident took place during a dinner in the King's presence.[34] The King inquired after Humbaracıbaşı (Head Bombardier) Ahmed Paşa, formerly the Comte de Bonneval. Bonneval had come to the Ottoman Empire in 1729 and, after converting to Islam, had joined the Ottoman army. He had been a well-known general in the French and Austrian armies.[35] The King said that Bonneval had been his companion in battles; Bonneval's skills in battle could only be matched by at most two or three men in the entire West (Frengistan).[36]

The other incident occurred on Mehmed Said Efendi's return voyage.

When Mehmed Said was passing through Poland, the Polish King Augustus II died in February 1733.[37] The King's son and the father-in-law of Louis XV became the two pretenders to the throne. The French King requested that the Porte support Lezchinsky against Augustus III, who was the candidate of the Russians. Mehmed Said Efendi observed the situation in detail,[38] and reported on the imminent danger of a Russian invasion of Poland over the succession. The information he provided shaped Ottoman policy toward the problem of succession.

These embassy accounts contain a wealth of information on Ottoman society and on Ottoman perceptions of the West. The Ottomans regarded the embassy to Paris as crucial for their purposes and that embassy had the greatest impact on Ottoman society. The process through which this impact penetrated Ottoman society was complex. Western commercial expansion and technological development increased the Western pressure on Ottoman society. Ottoman social groups played the crucial role in absorbing, transforming, and diffusing this Western impact into Ottoman society. The rise of Western influence in Ottoman society had begun.

III

Factors Affecting the Spread of
Western Impact in
Ottoman Society

6

Commerce

La France cette suite [jeunes de Langues] de bons serviteurs, d'hommes remarquables, de patriotes dévoués, de royalistes épouves, de catholiques convaınçus qui, pendant tout le dix-huitième siècle, porterent haut dans tout l'Orient le pavillion Français.[1]

Commerce and the transmission of technology between the Ottoman Empire and the West was redefined in the eighteenth century. Between the fifteenth and seventeenth centuries, important changes took place in the West. Europeans devised a secular rational outlook. This outlook promoted scientific discoveries and produced technological, industrial, and agricultural revolutions. The Western economic system became more flexible. Centralized monarchies rose to organize and direct these developments. The West, armed with such developments, started to explore overseas, to colonize different parts of the world, and to expand commercially to different markets.[2]

This Western expansion pattern has been the subject of many studies. The coalescence of motives and aims appears crucial in Western expansion.[3] The two motives that induced Westerners to move overseas were acquisitiveness and religious zeal. The aims of Westerners, shaped by these motives and the developments that were taking place in Europe, were "to serve God and His Majesty, to give light to those who were in darkness, and to grow rich, as all men desire to do."[4] These motives and aims caused, for the first time, a collaboration between three vital Western institutions: the religious, the political, and the economic. The expansion was promoted, justified, and facilitated concurrently by Divine Will, the King, and Prosperity. New lands discovered for trade purposes profited Western merchants. The Christian missionaries expanded their activities into these lands. Western rulers legitimized the expansion by their political authority and tried to expand their control over these new domains. This coalescence of the aims of three important institutions quickened the pace of Western expansion.

More and more people were needed to empower this expansive movement:

more and more Westerners interacted with or lived in foreign cultures. French travelers had always been present in the Middle East. In 1574, Pierre Lescalopier, a Frenchmen, had visited the Porte where the Grand Vezir told him he was very astonished at the French for "coming from such long distances, when they have no business to conduct, putting themselves through all this trouble with the expectation of pleasure."[5] During the eighteenth century, because of the increase in Western interest and expansion, especially by the French, the French travelers became more numerous and diverse. In the eighteenth century, beside merchants, ambassadors, and travelers, many official envoys traveled to the Ottoman Empire with the mission of searching for coins and medallions, gathering inscriptions.[6]

Among these travelers was Paul Lucas, a jeweler, a medal engraver and collector, and a physician, commissioned by the French King to "search for rarities of antiquity: medallions, engraved stones and other monuments which would enrich the Royal collection."[7] He returned with a hundred medallions and many Oriental manuscripts for the King.[8] Pontchartrain, a French noble with an interest in the French Academy, charged Pitton de Tournefort to enrich both the Royal collections and those of the Academy by collecting antiquities and manuscripts.[9] In 1728, Abbé Sevin collected Oriental manuscripts and books. He returned to Paris with no less than six hundred manuscripts purchased for the Royal Library.[10] Manuscripts on Christianity and Greek civilization, along with those in Ottoman, Persian, and Arabic were collected avidly. This combination of religious and cultural interests supported by the King led to the development of large royal collections and libraries.

This new communication medium accompanied the increasing French commercial interest in the Ottoman Empire. Western technological advances had led to the production of large quantities of goods. The large, affluent, accessible Ottoman market was ideal for the sale of these goods. Competition for the Ottoman market developed between the British and the French.[11] In the eighteenth century, French trade with the Ottoman Empire expanded to the detriment of the British. The French gained superiority over the British in the Ottoman market through reducing prices by ten percent.[12] By 1740, while the number of trade vessels the British sent to the Mediterranean was around ten, the French sent as many as seven hundred. Among the French exports, textiles were the most important, followed by the products of overseas possessions such as coral, sugar refined in France, spices, wine, tinctorials (to die cotton goods), Indigo of the Antilles, and cochineal.[13] The main French imports from the Ottoman Empire during 1717 to 1720 were cotton, wool, raw silk, oils, animal skin, wax, grain, rice, coffee, tobacco, and pharmaceuticals.[14] The French had totally penetrated the Ottoman market by the end of the eighteenth century; they had expanded into the Adriatic and the Black Sea regions, the Balkans, Asia Minor, Syria, Egypt, Persia and the Persian Gulf, and the Red Sea.[15] Many French consulates were also established throughout the Ottoman Empire to help facilitate French commerce. The French state attempted to regulate the expanding French trade with the Ottoman Empire by introducing sets of rules and regulations.[16]

The success of French commerce resulted from the cooperation between the French chambers of commerce and the French King. The Marseilles Chamber of Commerce was the most influential chamber of commerce during the eighteenth century. Although the French King officially appointed the French officials in the Ottoman Empire, the chambers of commerce often provided the funds. Before embarking for Constantinople on a vessel of the King, the French ambassador usually passed by Marseilles, conferred with the chamber of commerce, and received a set of instructions that supplemented the instructions of commerce received at Versailles.[17]

This cooperation of French political and economic interests helped enhance the French impact. Other than the French ambassador in Constantinople, the French consuls, vice-consuls, chancellors, and dragomans were scattered throughout the Ottoman Empire. There were general consuls, for example, in İzmir, Aleppo, Baghdad, Sayda, Egypt, Morea, Tripoli in North Africa, Tunisia, Algeria, and Morocco. Cyprus, Tripoli in Syria, and Salonica only had consulates. The recruitment and promotion of these consuls were also systematized during the eighteenth century.[18]

The French chambers of commerce, especially that of Marseilles, were very important in penetrating the Ottoman market during the seventeenth and early eighteenth centuries. The French need for more dragomans to aid the merchants in their transactions began to increase in the late seventeenth century. Correspondence in 1670 between M. de Colbert, the French minister, and Nointel, the French ambassador at the Porte, addressed this need.[19] The Ottoman dragomans employed by the French were insufficient in number, difficult to work with, and not protective of French interests in the transactions. Colbert had therefore decided to institute a practice of sending French youths between the ages of six and ten to Constantinople and İzmir. They would stay at the monasteries the Capuchin friars had established in these Ottoman cities and would be instructed in the Catholic religion and learn Middle Eastern languages to serve as French interpreters upon graduation. To realize this project, the King ordered the Marseilles chamber of commerce to pay three hundred livres for each youth every year to the Capuchin friars in return for food, expenses, and education.

This project of training compatriot youths as interpreters had been attempted before by other Western powers.[20] In 1557, the Senate of Venice had decided to send a few youths from Venice (*giovani della lingua*) to the Ottoman Empire to be trained as translators. The practice had coincided with the Venetian commercial ascendance in the Ottoman Empire and continued for a century. In the end, it had to be abandoned because of the inability of most youths to master Turkish properly. The native translators, because of their superior knowledge of Ottoman customs and traditions, also had more successful communication with the Ottomans.

The English made a similar attempt and attained similar results. The English Levant Company sent the sons of some Greek families to Oxford at the end of the seventeenth century. These men were educated as translators. When the British ambassador Sutton wanted to send a second group, however, he was refused by the Levant Company. The company had not seen any results in its endeavor and was therefore unwilling to continue the practice.

The French attempt was successful because the French economic, political, and religious interests coincided in support of the project. Through this project, the French state would increase its political influence and prestige in the Ottoman Empire.[21] The institutions established by the Capuchin friars in the Ottoman Empire to help educate the Catholics would also be supported through this project. It would also facilitate French commercial expansion.

The French project ran into some problems in practice. The Marseilles chamber of commerce did not want to finance it; the chamber did not wish to dispense with any part of its income accruing from French duties on imported oils.[22] After much dispute, the French state and the chamber negotiated that one-half percent of the duty would be spent for financing the project.[23] Though the chamber supported the project,[24] finances continued to be a problem since the chamber refused to compensate increasing project costs.

In 1670, the training of these youths began in Constantinople. The French referred to them as Jeunes de Langues, or "language youths." They were chosen from the French families living in France or in the Levant. The French state decided to establish a similar institution in Marseilles to train French youths and the sons of Greeks, Syrians, and Armenians in the Ottoman Empire. This project was not realized. Instead, under Louis XIV, Christian youths from the Ottoman Empire were placed in the College de Louis-le-Grand in Paris to be educated.[25] This college was run by Jesuits; it complemented the school in Constantinople run by Capuchin friars. After a rigorous training in Latin, Turkish, Arabic, and religious studies, these youths were sent out to the school in Constantinople to continue their education.[26]

The college[27] of Capuchins in Constantinople was at Pera, the quarter of foreign embassies. The Jeunes de Langues had an Ottoman religious scholar who taught them Arabic and Persian. They also had a master teaching Latin. There was no occasion for them to speak these languages, however. To practice their Turkish, they went to Ottoman coffee houses. Their entertainment consisted of taking walks in Constantinople, attending various activities such as recitals, dances, and theatre performances at the various Western embassies. In 1795, these two institutions were replaced by l'Ecole des Langues Orientales Vivant (School of Contemporary Middle Eastern Languages) in Paris.[28]

These institutions were important in intensifying relations between France and the Ottoman Empire. The youth in Constantinople enhanced the French presence there. Through their language skills, they made French culture more accessible to Ottoman society and French influence and commerce in the Ottoman Empire spread. The presence of these youths in France helped augment and enhance the field of Oriental Studies. Their demand for Oriental books helped revive the French presses printing such books.[29]

Ottoman reaction to Western technological development, exploration, and commercial expansion was weak. As the West expanded into the oceans, the Ottoman trade and control remained confined to the Mediterranean. The geographical position of the Ottoman Empire constrained its power. Strong Ottoman state control had facilitated Ottoman military expansion in the earlier centuries; during the eighteenth century, the strength of the Ottoman state inhibited an Ottoman reciprocation to the Western expansion. In the West, the wealth generated through trade had escaped state control and transformed Western economic relations. The Ottoman state control over wealth repressed such a development.

The Ottoman reaction to French commercial expansion consisted of an attempt to exploit trade privileges politically. Ottomans also tried to reshape parts of the Ottoman administrative structure to meet the increasing demands of Western expansion. Ottoman trade privileges given to the West became tools for political negotiation. The Ottomans tried to procure allies by granting trade privileges.[30] In 1690, they decreased the Egyptian customs duties for the French from ten to three percent when they wanted to win France to their side against Austria. After France made peace with Austria in 1697, the Ottomans tried to punish the French by giving the monopoly of the Egypt–Constantinople sea transportation to English merchants. This use of trade privileges as an Ottoman political weapon started working against the Ottomans in the eighteenth century. With Western ascendance, the Ottomans lost control over this weapon; they were forced to give out more and more trade privileges. The West, armed with many trade privileges, penetrated Ottoman markets with Western goods, merchants, and travelers.

The increasing Western strength affected the administrative orientation of the Ottoman Empire. The Ottoman military defeats and the growing need for diplomatic negotiations with the West enhanced the importance of Ottoman foreign relations. The rising importance of the Ottoman secretary in charge of foreign affairs documents this development. Between 1703 and 1774, six bureaucrats became Grand Vezirs; of these six, five had also served as the secretary in charge of foreign affairs. Ottoman administration was controlled more and more by ''men of the pen'' rather than by ''men of the sword.'' There was a gradual shift from a military to a bureaucratic empire.[31]

7

Technology

Since we were knocked out by cannon balls, naturally we became interested in them, thinking that by learning to make them we could strike back. . . . from studying cannon balls we came to mechanical inventions, which in turn led us to political reforms; for political reforms we began to see political theories, which led us again to the philosophies of the West. On the other hand, through mechanical inventions we saw science, from which we came to understand the scientific method and the scientific mind. Step by step we were led farther and farther away from the cannon ball—yet we came nearer and nearer to it.[1]

Behind Western commercial expansion and recurrent military victories was a new Western technology. This new technology redefined the relation between man, culture, and technology. The emergence and diffusion of technical innovations, such as firearms, the instruments of open-sea navigation, map making, printing, clockmaking, precision instruments, into the society—this particular pattern and process—defined the new Western technology.[2] This new technology acquired its own momentum; it altered the structure of Western society. The attempts to diffuse this technology to other cultures revealed how culture-bound technology was, how a technological product "had a practical meaning only as an expression of man's response to the problems set by his environment and by his fellow men."[3]

The Ottoman Empire had to borrow and adopt Western technological products to maintain Ottoman military power. Ottomans had been quick in appreciating the value of firearms; they used the cannon effectively in conquering Constantinople.[4] Western renegades and venturers provided most of the science and technology needed to produce guns. This Ottoman interest in guns also extended to mining, shipbuilding, and navigation. The other technological product imported by the Ottoman Empire throughout the centuries was the eyeglass. Although the exact date and place of the invention of the eyeglass are not known, it is said to have been invented in Pisa or Florence

103

during the early part of the fourteenth century.[5] Its spread to Iran as early as 1480 is traced through a poem.[6]

The West also made a contribution to the Ottomans in the science of medicine. Western medicine penetrated the Ottoman Empire through Ottoman minorities who were physicians; Western medical skills were also needed in the seventeenth century to cure an ailment that came from the West: syphilis.[7] Another substance from the West to penetrate the Ottoman Empire very quickly was tobacco. Tobacco had originated in the New World where Columbus encountered it being smoked by Cuban natives.[8] The plant, when it moved to Europe, was for a long time an object of curiosity. Tobacco started to be cultivated and smoked in Europe by the sixteenth century. The information on the spread of tobacco to the Ottoman Empire is fragmentary.[9] According to Peçevi,[10] Karaçelebizade,[11] and Katip Çelebi,[12] tobacco was brought to the Ottoman Empire during the first years of the seventeenth century. It was initially sold as a cure for "wet" diseases,[13] yet its general use spread very rapidly. Finding prevention impossible, the Ottoman state decided to discourage smoking by imposing a heavy customs duty on the buyer and seller in 1690.[14] From being an importer of tobacco, the Ottoman Empire became a great tobacco exporter by the end of the eighteenth century.

The initial Ottoman reactions to various Western technological developments reveal the differential impact of Western technology on a foreign culture. The adoption of new military technology was of central concern to the Ottomans. Yet, in the adoption of Western technology, besides military products, the Ottoman reaction to three Western technological products— clocks, textiles, and the printing press—reveals three different patterns of reaction to Western technological diffusion.

Clocks

The mechanical clock was very important in transforming the West. As a precision instrument, it systematized the passage of time and measured productivity and performance.[15] As a cultural instrument, with the evolution of clocks into watches, it made time portable and private; it provided an impetus for individualism.[16] As a precision instrument, it led to the development of the clockmaking profession in France, England, and Switzerland.

The diffusion of the mechanical clock to the Ottoman Empire was gradual. Although the mechanical clock was invented around 1300, at the same time as the eyeglass, the first document of interest regarding these inventions dates from 1477.[17] After the peace treaty of 1477, Mehmed II asked the Signoria of Venice to send him somebody to make "christallini." This request can be interpreted as a request for an export craftsman able to grind spectacles. The first documented Ottoman interest in watches dates from 1531.[18] A Venetian recounted that a gold ring with a watch on it, which he had seen in Venice, was bought by Sultan Süleyman I. These initial instances of Ottoman interest in watches impelled Western ambassadors to present clocks and watches as gifts to the Sultan to gain favors. Shortly after, local rulers and officials were also given clocks and watches besides the traditional gift of precious textiles.[19]

The quantity of clocks and watches in the Ottoman Empire rose after the agreement drawn up with Austria in 1547. This agreement stipulated the payment of a yearly tribute to the Ottoman Empire to deter Ottoman aggression.[20] The tribute was delicately referred to as "Türkenverehrung," the Turkish gift, by the Austrians. It consisted of a large sum of money, silver ornaments, and clocks. These objects, produced exclusively for the Ottomans, gradually created a market for clocks in the Ottoman Empire. Even after the cessation of the tribute, the market for Western clocks and ornaments persisted.

The correspondence between Western merchant watchmakers in the eighteenth century included long lists of clocks and watches that were being shipped to the Ottoman Empire.[21] During the eighteenth century the English, French, and Swiss watchmakers started to compete for the Ottoman market in watches and clocks. They attempted to cater to the Ottoman taste by adorning the clocks with Islamic dials, and with scenes on the cover from the Bosphorus or Mecca. The watchmakers even put their signatures on their products in Arabic script.[22]

Although these Western sources document the gradual emergence of an Ottoman market for clocks and watches, there is little information on the Ottoman receptivity and usage of these products. Ottoman miniatures sometimes depict ceremonies in which the valuable gifts given to the Sultan included clocks. Other valuable gifts included harnessed horses, Chinese vases, fur coats, and expensive cloths. The Topkapı Palace contains many clocks and watches acquired during the eighteenth century. One such clock, mounted to the base of a gold bird cage, depicts the ambiguous function of a clock within Ottoman society. The clock acquired a highly ornamental value in the Ottoman context. It did not have a spatial restriction; it could be mounted wherever one desired an ornament.

The clock was, for the Ottomans, the technological product of a foreign culture. One could therefore assume that the Ottoman response was similar to the well-documented Chinese response. When the Europeans brought over Western technological products, the Chinese response was uniform.

Lenses, clocks and other instruments that had been developed in Europe to satisfy specific needs felt by European society in response to problems set by the

European socio-cultural environment. . . . For the Chinese, these contrivances fell unexpectedly out of the blue and quite naturally the Chinese regarded them merely as amusing oddities.[23]

Ottomans might have reacted in a similar fashion. As life and work in the Ottoman Empire were regulated according to prayers, there was no need for a more specific measurement of time. The prayer times were established by natural cycles of the day.[24] The Ottomans did, however, attempt to build precision instruments during the early period of Ottoman expansion. Taqi ad-Din (1525–1585), an Ottoman astronomer who wrote a treatise on clockmaking, built an observatory in Constantinople. Yet the Sheik ul Islam had told the Sultan that "observing the stars would bring about disaster, and that no kingdom with an observatory had lasted for long."[25] Murad III heeded his advice and had the observatory destroyed. This was the only Ottoman attempt before the eighteenth century to reproduce the Western technological development in precision instruments and it failed. Precision instruments were thereafter imported from the West. The maintenance of these precision instruments in the Ottoman Empire was delegated to foreigners. Palace registers contain some information on the foreigners working in the Palace without specifying their functions.[26] Some of these foreigners were clockmakers.[27] In these registers, they were often listed together with palace artisans.[28]

The increase in Ottoman clock and watch use resulted in the formation of a group of foreigners in the Ottoman Empire. This group imported and repaired clocks and watches. In the late sixteenth century, there were "many German, English, French and Italian goldsmiths, clockmakers and gem engravers living in Galata, the quarter where foreigners resided; for the most part these people return to Europe as soon as they have made some money."[29] In the seventeenth century, this group was succeeded by a colony of Calvinist watchmakers from Geneva.[30] It had become a practice for young men from Geneva to go to Constantinople, work for a few years after their apprenticeship, and then return to Geneva. These watchmakers were under the protection of the French ambassador.[31]

A majority of the watches in the Ottoman Empire were imported from Geneva. Around 1650, some watchmakers in Constantinople put watches together on the spot from imported parts.[32] As watchmaking developed technologically in the West, watches started to be mass produced. The competitive prices of these Western mass-produced watches drove the costly assembled watches of Constantinople out of the market. Watchmaking by the colony of watchmakers in Galata lost its importance through this development in the eighteenth century. The Western competition in the Ottoman market thus inhibited Ottoman attempts to counter the West and reproduce clocks and watches in the Ottoman Empire.

Textiles

The Ottoman reaction to another Western technological product, textiles, was different. When the Ottomans observed a large increase in Ottoman textile imports in the eighteenth century, they tried to reduce these imports. They attempted to weave textiles similar to those imported from France. In 1703,[33] the Grand Vezir Rami Mehmed Paşa tried to establish looms for textile production to counter the imported French textiles. He brought artisans from Bursa and Salonica to Constantinople. These artisans were experts in silk cloth and broadcloth production. A change in Ottoman succession during this attempt obstructed any further development. The strict state control over production did not let Ottoman producers counteract the Western products by freely changing their production techniques. Only the Ottoman state had enough power to counteract Western developments. Policy changes from one Ottoman administration to another inhibited such developments.

The mercantilist policies of the West presented obstacles to Ottoman textile production as well. The West very carefully guarded technological information on textile production. A report of the Venetian bailo in 1730 illustrates this policy very vividly:

> Because of the revolutions at home a Scot went to . . . Venice where he learned how to weave. After going to Rome and Corfu, he finally came to Constantinople and presented two pieces of damask and satin to the vizier. At a chess game with the French ambassador, Bartolini heard about the vizier's depositing thirteen purses for thirteen weavers' frames and the Scot's instructing persons on how to weave damask with gold. Although Bartolini pretended not to have heard this item, he notified Ferro, the merchant. The latter and others came to the embassy the following morning and the Scot was summoned. Quoting the proverb "Necessity has no law," Bartolini . . . settled the Scot's debts; paid for his lodging, food, clothing, transportation and passport; and gave money to both him and his wife. Fearing punishment, the director of the factory had fled.[34]

This particular damask production would have endangered Venetian exports to the Ottoman Empire; the Venetian bailo acted to protect Venetian interests. The Ottoman attempt to overcome Western textile domination failed even though the Ottomans tried, without success, to acquire looms of their own. But even if the Ottomans had produced such products, they could not have competed with their Western counterparts. Western textiles were priced very competitively because of the continuous technical developments in production. The Ottomans could have only overcome this competition of inexpensive Western textiles by preventing their inflow into Ottoman markets. The Ottoman trade privileges given to the West prevented such an action.

Printing Press

The third technological product, the printing press, was different from the clocks and textiles in one important aspect; it was successfully reproduced in the Ottoman Empire. A number of reasons contributed to this success. Culturally, the Ottomans were very interested in manuscripts and books; especially during the Tulip Era, the Sultan and many Ottoman dignitaries were exchanging and collecting books and founding libraries. Consumption of books was never stigmatized the way consumption of expensive clocks or textiles was. Printing presses had already been established in the Ottoman Empire among the Ottoman minorities. The Ottomans could draw on the experiences of the Ottoman minorities in establishing their official printing press. Even though the press itself was a Western invention, the Ottomans took over a fair portion of the Ottoman market for books. Arabic books printed in the West for the Ottoman market were insufficient in quantity to saturate the market.

The Ottoman cultural interest in books was apparent during the eighteenth century. Sultan Ahmed III was personally interested in collecting books. An anonymous French account[35] gave information about an encounter with the Sultan where he

> was seated on his feet . . . the great reader that he was, [he] stretched his hand toward the two cases with windows of crystal where his history books were . . . where very unusual books [are], in all kinds of languages, handwritten, and in particular one hundred and twenty volumes of Constantine the Great, each one two arm spans high and about three hand spans wide, made of parchment so fine that it resembled silk, written in letters of gold and covered in gilded silver, with precious stones of an inestimable price and containing the Old and New Testament and other histories and Lives of Saints.

This account, though exaggerated, reflects the Sultan's interest in books. The Sultan's own correspondence with his Grand Vezir, Damad İbrahim Paşa, documents his interest in books more directly. In one letter,[36] the Sultan asked his Grand Vezir to procure one particular book: "the religious scholars in the Palace have informed me that this book is without match. It has been taken to Mirzazade Efendi to be sold. Have it brought to you and send it to me so I can have a look at it." In another decree,[37] the Sultan asked for a set of books in Adrianople to be brought to Constantinople. He had learned that there was a work in Arabic by Ayni on the history of sciences in the library of the Sultan Selim mosque in Adrianople. People were assigned to go to the library, gather all volumes of the work, wrap them in two to three layers of wax-cloth to protect them from the cold weather, and place them in strong cases to guard against the dampness of the roads. The volumes could then be sent to Constantinople.

The Sultan was also concerned about the unavailability of some Palace books to the reader. In a note, he wanted the Grand Vezir to obtain a legal decision on the procedure to follow with the books of his predecessor Mustafa II.[38] He wrote

> My predecessor has collected and stored many books in the Treasury. . . . The Arabic books, commentaries on the Qur'an and traditions of the Prophet have been selected and are about to be donated to the library, to Galata, and some other places. Yet there is still a large number of books in Persian, Arabic, and Turkish. It is certainly a sin to leave these books neglected. Yet my predecessor has placed them as such. Is it appropriate for these to stay as placed or to be endowed to the people[?]

The concern of the Sultan for making the books available for public use required him to consult religious authorities. These authorities checked the public use of books; they controlled the dissemination of public information. They did not intervene in private information; the contents of private libraries were not questioned. The moment these private libraries were endowed for public use, however, the religious authorities closely scrutinized the contents of the books. Only religious books were permitted to be endowed for public use. The nonreligious books were sold out by Ottoman collectors.

The legal decision on the distribution of the books belonging to the late Şehid Ali Paşa[39] documents this policy. There are two imperial decrees of 1716[40] pertaining to the private library of the Paşa. One stated that the Paşa had endowed his property including the books in his personal library. Yet the religious opinion on the legal matter (of endowment) had declared that books filled with lies, namely those on history, poetry, astronomy, and philosophy, could not be included in an endowment. The decree asked for a register of these unfit books to be drawn, sealed, and sent to the Sultan. The other decree contained the decision on these registered books. Books that had been marked on the register were to be sent to the Palace. The others were to be priced and sold. Each day as many books as would be sold during a day would be taken out of the chest containing the books and be sold either at the mosque courtyard or the market. The decree also noted that the number of books contained in the register should not decrease beyond those sold as directed; they should not be illegally changed with other books, or given to some Ottoman dignitaries for protection. The Ottoman readers privately had access to books on all topics through these sales; they could easily purchase books that were decreed inappropriate for an endowment on religious grounds.

The contents of the private library of one Ottoman owner prove that the readers indeed had access to a variety of books. The French traveler Sevin who was in Constantinople during the first quarter of the eighteenth century recounted his meeting with an Ottoman, Mustafa Efendi, who was a great amateur of astronomy.[41] Mustafa Efendi wanted to present Sevin with twenty-two volumes in Arabic. Seven of these were on the history of Egypt and the rest were translations of various Greek astronomers and mathematicians. Sevin was tempted but resisted knowing that "Moslems do not give anything without expectation to receive the triple."

During the eighteenth century, libraries in the Ottoman Empire consisted of those in mosques and schools, those in the Palace, and those private or endowed libraries of the Ottoman dignitaries. In Constantinople, there were at least twenty-four libraries by the year 1730.[42] Ottoman society showed an interest in, was acquainted with, and had access to books. The Ottoman printing press evolved against this background.

The printing presses in the West started printing religious books in Arabic script by the sixteenth century for religious and trade purposes.[43] The first known Islamic book printed in the West was an Arabic book on the canonical times of prayer; this book was printed in 1514 at Fano (Italy) under the patronage of Pope Julius II. Two years later, in Genoa, an edition of the Psalms of David was printed in Hebrew, Greek, Arabic, Aramaic, and Latin. These books served to maintain the faith among the Arabic-speaking Christian communities in the Middle East and to help spread Christianity among other groups.

The printing of the Qur'an in Arabic in Venice as early as 1530 revealed a motive other than missionary activity—that of trade. In the sixteenth and seventeenth centuries, three noted Arabic printers existed in Italy.[44] The Medici Press published Gospels, Arabic grammar, Greek authors in Arabic translation, and a number of Islamic scientific works. The Arabic printing press founded by the Congregation for the Propagation of the Faith printed Arabic translations of the Bible and other Christian works. The outstanding product of Tipografia del Seminario in Padua was the publication of the Qur'an with an Arabic text and a Latin translation. These books were marketed in the Ottoman Empire.

Various Ottoman official documents reveal the Ottoman reaction to these printed books. An Ottoman imperial decree during the reign of Murad III in 1587–1588[45] confirms the trade purpose. Two merchants, Anton and Orasyo (Orazio), son of Bandini, from the West, had brought some goods and valuable printed books and treatises in Arabic, Persian, and Turkish to trade in the Ottoman Empire. Some people, "questioning the possession of Arabic, Persian, and Turkish books by these merchants (who were infidels)," took these books away from them by force. The Sultan ordered these people to give back the books. Another Ottoman petition by a foreigner during the reign of Murad

III requested a license[46] to print a book with Turkish letters for trade purposes and to be exempt from customs duties in marketing it. The license was granted and *Usul ül aklidis* (*Euclidean Principles*) was printed in 1587 for commercial purposes. The Ottoman state was favorable to the trade and printing of books by foreigners in the Ottoman Empire.

The printing presses of the minorities in the Ottoman Empire might have generated this favorable response from the state. Book printing was brought to the Ottoman Empire from the West in the fifteenth century by Jewish exiles from Spain and Portugal.[47] These presses were authorized by the Ottoman state to print "only in either Hebrew or Latin characters, thus offering no threat to either prejudice or interest."[48] In 1494, David ben Nahmiyas and his brother Shemuel established the first printing press in Constantinople and printed *Arba'ah Turim* (*Four Columns*) of Rabbi Ya'akov ben Asher. The Nahmiyas printing press continued into the sixteenth century. The Soncino's, who had established printing houses throughout Italy, branched out to the Ottoman Empire and established presses in Salonika in 1527 and in Constantinople in 1530. In 1560, the Ja'abez brothers founded a printing press in Constantinople and produced a series of rabbinic, philosophical, anti-Christian, and Karaite works until 1586. The next Hebrew press in Constantinople was established in 1593 by Joseph Nasi's widow Dona Reyna Nasi; it continued publication for five years before running into financial difficulties and closing down. Approximately two hundred Hebrew books were printed in Constantinople and Salonika during the sixteenth century. In 1638, Shelomo Franco set up a press with his son Abraham and his son-in-law Ya'akov Gabbai; the son Abraham, who employed several refugees from the Chmielnicki massacres, continued printing until 1683. At the beginning of the eighteenth century, Jonah ben Jacob set up a press in Constantinople. Most of the printed books were rabbinic novellae, responsa, and homiletics.

The priest Apkar from Sivas was the founder of the first Armenian printing press in the Ottoman Empire.[49] He came to Constantinople in 1567 after learning the art of printing in Venice and started the first Armenian printing press at the endowed estates of the Serbian Nigogus church in Kumkapı. A book on the Armenian language was the first product of this Armenian press; it was followed by a prayer book in 1568. The next official reference to the Armenian printing press is a century later in 1698.[50] In accordance with a decree from the Sultan, a printing press imported by the Armenians was destroyed by the Janissaries soon after its arrival.

The first Greek printing press in the Ottoman Empire was founded in the seventeenth century by a priest from Kafalonya, Nikodemus Metaxas.[51] In 1627, with the aid of the Greek patriarch Kirilyos Lukaris, Greeks in Constantinople brought supplies from London and founded a Greek printing press. The Jesuits strongly opposed this undertaking. The priest had to move the printing press to the English embassy to have secure working conditions. Because of mounting Jesuit opposition, the press was destroyed in 1628 by the Janissaries.

The reaction of the Ottoman state to these printing presses was uneven; some presses and publications were allowed to circulate publications while others were rapidly destroyed. The first document on the Ottoman reaction is a decree of Bayazıd II renewed by Selim I in 1515 which states that "occupying oneself with the science of printing was punishable by death."[52] This order might indicate the Ottoman reservations about the printing press as a dangerous instrument for communication.

Two decrees in 1720 and 1721[53] refer to the social disturbances kindled because of a printing press. Armenian priests in the Ottoman Empire attempted to Catholicize the Ottoman Armenian community; they spread their works through an Armenian printing press. The first decree was addressed to the head official in Constantinople.

> In two locations in Galata and in the inn of Validehanı, some mischief-makers have begotten new prints. They reprint Armenian books with alterations and additions. The malice and villainy [intended by these people] have become evident through the disturbances and the splits caused among the Armenian people upon the spread of these books. [You should] get hold of these people in any event, imprison them, and notify my Porte about the state of the case.

The second decree clarifies this alleged use of priests to convert Armenians to Catholicism and was the Porte's response after being notified of the circumstances of the case. The decree was again addressed to the head official of Constantinople.

> You have communicated in detail that . . . a priest Hacador who tempted, corrupted, and encouraged the Armenian people to [change to] the creeds of the Europeans was captured and sent to the prison of the galley slaves . . . that when the book printers were inspected, none were reprimanded since they had a current permit for printing books between them . . . and that the false printed books came from Europe and were sold through the mediation of those scoundrels who obeyed [the false books]. [I order you] to imprison Hacador in the galleys . . . to discover with scrutiny all such book printers wherever they are, in the inns Validehanı and Vezirhanı or elsewhere, and burn their tools and annul their workshops (permits) since this type of printing is innovative and perverse. . . . to strictly warn and reiterate your warning to them henceforth not to let one single person print (such books) . . . and henceforth to imprison them and notify my Porte in full detail if they are not cautious and dare to print (such) books.

This "innovative and perverse type of printing" must have been seen by the Ottoman state as demonstrating the seditious effects of printed books on religious issues.[54]

The unfavorable opinions of those Ottomans who resisted the foundation of an Ottoman printing press five years later could have been influenced by this particular usage of the printing press. An item of correspondence of İbrahim Müteferrika, who founded the Ottoman printing press in 1726, adds support to this possibility. In his letter to De Saussure,[55] Müteferrika stated that "the religious dignitaries, who possess influence in this country, insistently did not give permission for this new invention. . . . They have mentioned that the aforesaid invention would be dangerous to public order and to the conduct of religion; it would place more than the necessary amount of books into circulation." Their fears were well-grounded. The printing press as a new medium of communication disseminated knowledge and information. It gradually broke the monopoly of religious dignitaries.

To counter the effects of the Ottoman opposition, İbrahim Müteferrika composed a treatise for Sultan Ahmed III on the advantages of the printing press.[56] After emphasizing the educational value of books as well as their function in spreading knowledge, İbrahim emphasized practical consequences. The print would be durable and of uniformly high quality. The attached table of contents would facilitate references to the books. The scrutiny of the board of proofreaders would eliminate the frequent copying mistakes of manuscripts. The end product would be a definite improvement over the European prints in Arabic script that were filled with errors. A large quantity of printed books would ensure profits and lower prices so the Ottoman populace could afford to buy books. The cheapness would permit the populace of the provinces to purchase these books as well. People studying science would increase with the growing number of books and libraries in the cities. Such an act would thus benefit all Moslems.

As a result of these discussions, İbrahim Müteferrika, a Hungarian seminarist who became a convert, and Mehmed Said Efendi, son of the Ottoman ambassador Yirmisekiz Çelebi Mehmed Efendi, were granted permission in 1726 to establish an Ottoman printing press, and to print, for the first time, books in Turkish in the Ottoman Empire.[57] The first book printed in the Ottoman Empire in Arabic script had been printed in 1706 in Aleppo. With the encouragement of the Patriarch of Antioch, a priest Asnagof who had come from a Wallachian monastery printed the Bible by pressing pages engraved in wood onto paper.[58] The permission given to İbrahim Müteferrika and Mehmed Said Efendi specifically excluded the printing of religious books.

The history of the Ottoman printing press can be reconstructed from Ottoman, Turkish, and French sources. Previous to its official recognition in 1726, İbrahim Müteferrika and Mehmed Said Efendi worked privately for two years to establish the printing press; Mehmed Said Efendi financed the endeavor. İbrahim Müteferrika was able to attach a sample of two printed pages of their first book[59] to his official request for permission to print five hundred copies. The sample pages from the first book were also sent by Mehmed Said Efendi to Abbé Bignon, librarian of King Louis XV. The Abbé had been corresponding with Said Efendi with the hope of gaining access to the Topkapı Palace libraries.[60] After receiving the samples, the Abbé asked for copies of all the books printed by the Ottoman press.

The first printed Ottoman book was one of the classical Arabic dictionaries of the tenth century, *al-Sihah*, of al-Jauhari.[61] The Ottomans referred to it as the *Vankulu* dictionary because it was translated into Ottoman by a certain Mehmed Efendi, a former judge of Medina, who had been nicknamed Van Kulu, as he was from the Van region.[62] The Vankulu dictionary was on sale in 1729 in two volumes.[63] Its price was determined as thirty-five *guruş* per volume.[64] The second book, by Katip Çelebi, was printed four months later. The following year, a Jesuit missionary in Constantinople, P. Holdermann, obtained permission to print a grammar book at the Ottoman printing press. The Turkish and French grammar book was for the use of Jeunes de Langues and all French merchants in the Ottoman Empire.[65]

Said Efendi lost his interest in the printing press at this point. In 1729, the French traveler Fourmont narrated his visit to the Ottoman printing press in a letter. He mentioned that "Said Efendi's interest in the press had decreased; other than Müteferrika, who was knowledgeable in printing, the press was run by a wretched Polish Jew who knew very little Turkish."[66] The press was briefly closed down during the Patrona revolt of 1730. When it reopened in 1732, it was registered under İbrahim Müteferrika's name since Said Efendi had left their partnership.[67]

The next reference to the printing press is in a decree of 1741[68] that determined the prices of two newly printed books, the chronicles of Raşid and Çelebizade Asım. The prices were thirty *guruş* for each unbound volume, and forty *guruş* for each bound volume. In 1747, the lease of the press changed hands on İbrahim Müteferrika's death.[69] The lease was given to İbrahim Efendi and Ahmed Efendi on the condition that they "continue the practice and replenishment of the science of printing."

The identities of the people working the press and the origins of the tools used in it are difficult to trace. Different explanations exist for the source of the Ottoman letters cast for the printing press. Various accounts point to Vienna or Paris; some others state that the letters were cast in Constantinople. Some correspondence by İbrahim Müteferrika substantiates the latter statement; the letters were cast in Constantinople probably by an Ottoman Jew.[70] İbrahim Müteferrika applied for a warrant for exemption from the Ottoman poll-tax for an Ottoman Jew and his son working in the printing press. He stated that "he has profited from the services of the Jew named Yuna, who possesses all the important elements [needed for printing], is knowledgeable in the art of printing, and is an expert in the art of tools, implements, and requisites." The service provided by this Jew may be the reason for Müteferrika's confidence in another letter where he stated[71] that "various forms of calligraphy such as *nesih, ta'lik* will be produced in the shortest time."

In 1744, an Ottoman paper mill was established by İbrahim Müteferrika to produce paper for the printing press.[72] Müteferrika sent an Ottoman Jew to Poland to procure three experts. These Polish experts had a one-year contract with the Ottoman state to teach their professions; they were to receive forty *akças* per day and a three-hundred *guruş* bonus.[73]

This paper mill was located in Yalakabad (Yalova) near Constantinople. A geography book compiled by Hamid Efendi around 1748 refers to the purchase by one Hacı Mustafa Ağa in 1741–1742 of a farm "where the mill kiln [was used] by paper-masters who were brought from Europe through the mediation of a person by the name of İbrahim the printer . . . where iron mortars were made over water and a paper mill was formed."[74] Two orders in 1745 and 1746 to the deputy judge of Yalakabad declared the Ottoman minorities "who organize and regulate the course of the river running through the paper mill" tax-exempt.[75] This paper mill, established to supply the Ottoman printing press, indicated the gradual expansion of the technological product into Ottoman society. The Ottoman minorities, especially Jews, played a crucial role in this establishment.

8

Social Groups
in Ottoman Society

The transformation of Western impact into long-term Western influence was a complex process. Western influence can be defined as the penetration and diffusion of the Western impact into Ottoman society. Western commercial and technological expansion produced and maintained the Western impact on Ottoman society. Yet, when the Ottoman society in Constantinople is analyzed during the eighteenth century, the crucial role of Ottoman social groups in diffusing the Western impact into Ottoman society emerges.

The capital city of Constantinople facilitated the communication between the Ottoman Empire and the West. It was an easily accessible port city joined with many diverse regions by sea routes.[1] Constantinople was also located on land routes between Asia and Europe, which guaranteed its establishment as an economic and commercial center. The residence of the Ottoman Sultan in Constantinople further defined the city as an administrative and political center. These concentrations of functions in Constantinople led to a constant population increase.

According to the Ottoman imperial decrees, the population of the city grew rapidly during and after the eighteenth century. It is very difficult to assess this population. Frequent Ottoman registers drawn up for tax purposes included only males and household heads. There were around forty-five thousand Christians and eight thousand Jews paying the poll-tax in 1690. Women, children, students, Ottoman dignitaries, and others exempted from taxes for providing public services were not included in these figures. In 1669, approximately twenty thousand palace personnel, eighty thousand troops, and forty thousand Janissaries were in Constantinople. The total population of Constantinople was estimated to be around seven or eight hundred thousand.[2] Constantinople started becoming too attractive during and after the eighteenth century according to the imperial decrees. A decree of 1732[3] tried to stop the flow of people from towns and villages in Rumelia and Anatolia to Constantinople. Such decrees were repeated frequently through that century and later ones. The increased population density in Constantinople intensified the communication between inhabitants of the city.[4] The inhabitants of Constantinople, located at the center of the Empire, set the tone for Ottoman society.[5]

These inhabitants were very diverse; there were travelers, scholars, merchants from all parts of the Ottoman Empire, in addition to slaves, travelers, ambassadors from all over the world. The presence of Western residents in Constantinople was important for the dissemination of Western influence into Ottoman society.

Foreign Residents

Westerners had an important colony in Constantinople even before the Ottoman conquest of the city. They represented and personified the West to the East. The fifteenth-century description of the city by Tursun Bey right before the Ottoman conquest emphasized this role of Westerners:[6]

> [He is describing the castle of Constantinople] . . . again on the Black Sea side at the entrance of the harbor, opposite the castle of Constantinople, a castle named Kal'ata (Galata) had been constructed in a triangular form; it is wide, spacious, and filled with Christians. It has been in the possession of the offensive Western rulers. It is a strange thing that due to the abundance of boatmen with vessels, one person can [cross between the sides] and watch, with a *mangır* eight of which make an *akça,* Europe from Asia Minor and Asia Minor from Europe.

This cosmopolitan character of the city was maintained during the Ottoman period. Constantinople was repopulated by Sultan Mehmed II (1451–1480) with Greeks, Jews, Armenians, and Turks.[7] The size of the non-Moslem population was noticed by many travelers. In the late seventeenth century, the suburbs of Galata and Pera had substantial non-Moslem populations. Evliya Çelebi counted seventeen Moslem districts, seventy Greek districts, three Frankish districts, two Armenian districts, and one Jewish district in the suburb of Galata.[8]

During the seventeenth century, the adjoining suburb of Pera also started to develop as foreign embassies were established. The establishment of these embassies signified an important change in Western diplomatic representation in the Ottoman Empire. In the preceding centuries, Western merchants had been the official economic representatives of Western states to the Ottoman Empire. In the seventeenth century, merchants were replaced by special consuls and ambassadors as Western state control over commerce increased. These consuls and ambassadors became the official state representatives and established official residences.[9] The ambassadors were also paid by the Western states, unlike the merchants who had been paid by Western trade companies.

This development changed the character of the Western community in the Ottoman Empire. The new residents had an interest in the social and political life of Ottoman society. They did not restrict their attention to trade relations. Ambassadors and consuls described life in the Ottoman Empire in detailed embassy reports. These reports, and the experiences of the people with them or visiting them, helped foster a Western interest in the Ottoman Empire.

These gradual changes in the characteristics of foreign residents and their lives in Constantinople can be documented through the description of the Austrian embassy.[10] The character of Austrian embassies in Constantinople changed rapidly between the sixteenth and eighteenth centuries. The ambassadors had initially been chosen from among soldiers who knew frontier life well. Later, lawyers and humanists from aristocratic families were appointed as Austrian ambassadors to the Porte.[11]

The retinue of an ambassador consisted of one or two scribes, with one an expert in coding, one translator, one courier, painters as visual correspondents, clergy for religious observance, physicians, pharmacists, barbers for health reasons, and servants, grooms, and coach drivers. In all, there were between twenty and thirty embassy personnel.[12] After the seventeenth century, however, the number of embassy personnel increased rapidly as the Austrian aristocrats brought their own large retinues. Many Western travelers also accompanied ambassadors to Constantinople to see the Ottoman Empire. The changing transportation requirements of ambassadors seem to reflect the vast increase in the size of the embassies. In 1699, Ambassador Ottingen needed forty-two vessels to make the trip from Venice to Constantinople whereas Ambassador Virmond in 1718 had to request seventy-two vessels for the same trip.

The increased Western presence in the Ottoman Empire during the eighteenth century should have, in theory, increased communication between the Westerners and Ottoman society. The communication between the Westerners and Ottoman society was very restricted, however. The Ottoman state considered Westerners as agents and spies, and regarded all their actions with suspicion. The actions of the Westerners were controlled by the Ottoman state through the assignment of Janissary units to each embassy for their protection. These Janissaries were also required to accompany foreign residents continually outside the embassy. This measure restricted the communication between Westerners and Ottomans.

Eighteenth-century miniatures sometimes portrayed the foreign residents of Constantinople. In depictions of Ottoman public festivals, foreign residents were easily recognizable by their distinctive modes of dress.[13] These foreigners were often set apart in a separate tent; no Ottomans stood even close to the tent. These foreign residents sat on chairs, unlike the Ottomans who sat on cushions. Their dragomans as well as their Janissary guards always accompanied them.

Beside the restrictions imposed by the Ottoman state, language and religion formed natural barriers to the foreign residents' communication with Ottoman society. The enmity between Christianity and Islam, accompanied by the political conflicts between the Western powers and the Ottoman Empire, reflected negatively on the relations between Westerners and Ottomans. Language was another formidable obstacle. Foreigners needed the mediation of a very significant group in Ottoman society, Ottoman minorities, in all their communications with Ottoman society. As the Western presence in the Ottoman Empire increased, more and more Ottoman minorities were drawn into positions as intermediaries between the West and the Ottoman Empire.

Ottoman Minorities

The minorities in the Ottoman Empire consisted mainly of Jews, Armenians, Greeks, and Arab Christians. Their special position in Ottoman society was defined by Islamic law and practice. The minorities paid higher taxes; they also faced restrictions on the clothes they wore, the beasts they rode, and the buildings they built.[14] These restrictions were not always imposed, however; they existed in principle. Ottoman minorities specialized in a variety of occupations; some were in commerce and finance, the practice of medicine, and government service, but the majority were poor artisans and peasants.

The Jewish community was successful in trade, medicine, and government service during the sixteenth and seventeenth centuries.[15] Some Ottoman Jews were brokers for the Ottoman administration in customs duties and tax collection. These positions required knowledge of banking and money changing.[16] There were also prominent Jewish physicians.[17] The Palace registers contain frequent bestowals of money and cloaks to such Jewish physicians. In 1506, for example, the physicians Abraham and Joseph each received three thousand *akças* and a cloak from the Treasury.[18]

Overleaf. Ottoman festival during the reign of Sultan Ahmed III depicting the foreign residents of Constantinople. The foreign residents, who are watching the procession, are located at upper right-hand corner of the left page. The seated Sultan is at the upper right-hand corner of the right page. The miniature is in Topkapı Museum Library, Catalogue No. A3593, folios 139b and 140a. (*Courtesy of the Topkapı Museum Library, Istanbul*)

120

121

Ottoman Jews had started to lose their positions of influence during the eighteenth century. The one exception in Ottoman society where the Jews retained their position was within the Janissary organization. The position of supply purchaser for the Janissaries was held by Jews until the nineteenth century.[19] In their relations with the Westerners in the Ottoman Empire, Jews lost ground to Ottoman Greeks and Armenians who were of the same religion as Western residents. Jewish contacts with the West had also started to lose their importance. Their contacts had been in Italy which no longer was a major commercial center. Jews could not shift their contacts to central and eastern Europe because of the Ashkenazi-Sephardic differences between the Jews of south and north Europe.[20]

The Ottoman expansion during the eighteenth century to formerly Persian-held territory had increased Ottoman trade with the East. Armenians, who had established themselves as merchants and tradesmen along the route from Persia to Constantinople, gained influence because of this expansion of Ottoman trade.[21] As the Armenian community in Constantinople grew, some of its members started acquiring influence with the Ottoman administration.[22] Armenians also maintained ethnic and family ties in eastern Europe and sent their sons to be educated in Western universities. As Christians, they were preferred over Jews as translators and intermediaries[23] because they belonged to the same faith as most Westerners. The importance of Armenians as an Ottoman minority group increased during the eighteenth century.

The Ottoman Greek community was the largest group among the Ottoman minorities. It was also the group most closely involved with Western embassies.[24] Greeks benefited from rising Western presence. They enjoyed patronage from the Christians of Europe, sent their sons to Western universities, and cultivated Western ties.[25] They also improved their position by serving as agents in the provinces for Western merchants, by supplying goods from the Black Sea region where the Westerners did not have access, and by dealing in forbidden merchandise such as wheat and ancient coins.[26] In the late seventeenth century, the Phanariot Greeks established virtual autonomy as interpreters at the Porte to the detriment of other Ottoman minority groups.[27] This special group of translators within the Greek community will be discussed later in greater detail because of its special relation with the Ottoman state.

The relations between the minorities and the West were recognized and utilized by the Ottoman state. The Ottoman state employed many members of the minorities as translators in the Palace and in the foreign embassies. The Palace registers contain frequent references to such dragomans. In 1503, two dragomans, Alaeddin and İskender, received one thousand akças each on one occasion, and Alaeddin, İbrahim, and İskender received one thousand akças each on another occasion during the same year.[28]

The most important relationship between the Western residents and minorities evolved in conjunction with Western commercial expansion. More and more men from the Ottoman minorities were employed as translators. Procedurally, the ambassador applied to the Porte and requested a warrant for the person he wanted to employ. The fee for this warrant was paid in terms of gifts.[29] The warrant provided the minorities with immunity from taxes and with privileges in trade.[30] With this warrant, the Ottoman minorities were placed under Western protection and acquired, for the first time, a special status beyond the control of the Ottoman state.

The differential trade privileges that had been given by the Ottoman state to Ottoman minorities and Western merchants induced the minorities with warrants to engage in trade.[31] Western merchants in Ottoman territories had to pay a three percent customs duty whereas the Ottoman minority merchants were charged five percent. With the other additional taxes they had to pay, the tax of minorities rose to as much as ten percent. Under these conditions, several Ottoman minorities tried to get Western protection. Many got this chance to be recruited by the embassies as the expansion of Western trade increased the number of Western representatives in the Ottoman Empire. Some Ottoman minorities even paid large bribes to the ambassadors in Constantinople for warrants. Ambassadors sometimes created fictitious consulates throughout the Ottoman Empire to obtain more warrants from the Ottoman state.[32]

From the beginning of the eighteenth century, the Ottoman state tried to limit and control these warrants. The warrants both decreased the tax revenues and challenged the Ottoman state authority. The decrees of Sultan Ahmed III start to describe this situation and to try to remedy it. On June 1722, a decree dealt specifically with the exploitation of warrants.[33]

> Some Jews and Christians who have for many generations been the subjects of this exalted [Ottoman] State get a translator's warrant, which has strong economic powers, through some means or another to trade and to free their relatives and relations from the poll-tax. . . . Innumerable numbers gain translator status and transgress the usual limit. [In addition] they employ large numbers of others in their service. . . . These developments cause disturbance in the collection of the poll-tax and bring great damage to the Treasury of the Moslems.

In spite of numerous efforts by the Ottoman state to control the number of warrants, the misuse continued throughout the century. Similar decrees of Mustafa III (1757–1774) ascertain the seriousness of the problem for the Ottoman state. The revenues of the state as well as its authority over its own subjects were declining. This development was tied to the trade privileges of the Western powers; the Ottoman state could not stop this decline without disrupting trade privileges. The balance of powers in the eighteenth century ruled out any possibilities of the Ottoman state curbing Western trade privileges. The Ottoman state gradually lost its authority over Ottoman minorities. With increasing Western political power, the special status of Ottoman minorities with warrants was extended to cover large communities.

The close association between Ottoman minorities and Western residents in Constantinople expanded Western impact among the minorities very rapidly. In addition to the abuse of warrants, the Ottoman minorities disturbed the Ottoman state by changing the attire they had traditionally been assigned. They started imitating Western styles of dress. An imperial decree of 1758[34] banned the minorities from "wearing Western style clothing" as "this abominable situation disturbed the order among the subjects."

The imitation of Western manners by the Ottoman minorities was described by Baron de Tott.[35] He had been invited to a reception at the house of "Madame the First Dragoman" in 1760. He described the reception:

> A circular table, with chairs all around it, spoons, forks—nothing was missing except the habit of using them. But they did not wish to omit any of our manners which were just becoming fashionable among the Greeks as English manners are among ourselves, and I saw one woman throughout the dinner taking olives with her fingers and then impaling them on her fork in order to eat them in the French manner.

The Ottoman minorities were the first social group to assimilate to the West.

Ottoman minorities could not spread this Western impact to the rest of Ottoman society. The Ottoman state had placed restrictions on their communication. The most important restriction entailed housing; Ottoman minorities could not reside near mosques, and could not build houses more than two stories high.[36] This removal from neighborhoods around mosques implied a removal from Moslem neighborhoods which were centered around mosques. A decree in 1700[37] stated that Christians had bought or rented houses near a mosque. This situation had resulted "in a contraction among the congregation of the mosque." The inhabitants were therefore prohibited from renting or selling houses to Christians in this neighborhood. By a decree of 1726,[38] Jews near Yeni Cami were removed for "causing many abominable situations near the mosque." The decree stated that these houses be bought by Moslems "at fair market prices."

Ottoman minorities formed their own neighborhoods around their own churches or synagogues. Because of their specific religious practices, the minorities gravitated toward the areas settled by the foreign embassies as the Moslems moved away from these areas. Galata and Pera became the two important residential districts for foreign residents and Ottoman minorities. This proximity helped intensify the Western impact among the Ottoman minorities. Restrictions forced on the minorities by the Ottoman state, however, minimized their communication with the rest of Ottoman society. Their transmission of the Western impact to the rest of Ottoman society was inhibited.

One special group among the Ottoman minorities surmounted these restrictions and associated with Ottoman dignitaries. This group consisted of the Greek Phanariots. Originally, they were translators at the Porte; their influence as a group increased as they monopolized the translation positions. The name Phanariot indicated that they resided in the district of Phanar in Constantinople. Their status in Ottoman society changed when the Porte started to appoint them as governors to the Danubian principalities.

These appointments elevated the status of the Phanariots. As appointed governors, they were received ceremoniously by the Porte, bestowed a robe of honor and the honorary title of "bey" or prince. They then proceeded to the principality with their retinue and an Ottoman state delegation of approximately forty people. Their responsibilities consisted of ruling the principality, collecting taxes, spying on adjoining territories, and joining Ottoman campaigns in the West with their infantry and cavalry.[39]

These Phanariots had less difficulty in communicating with the rest of Ottoman society, especially the upper echelons, because of their high administrative status. The status of their relatives and households was also elevated by association. As these appointments became hereditary, influential lineages developed. The Phanariots came to hold a unique position in Ottoman society between the Ottoman and the Western cultures; they became educated in both and symbolized a special synthesis between the East and the West. As a social group, they played a crucial role in transmitting the Western impact to the Ottoman dignitaries.

Very little is known about this unique social group. The life of one of the members is well documented, however. The lives of Phanariots and their communication with Ottoman society can be reconstructed through studying the life of this member, Demetrius Cantemir, in the eighteenth century.[40] Demetrius Cantemir came to Constantinople in 1688 at the age of fifteen while his father, Constantine Cantemir, was serving as the Prince of Moldavia (1685–1693). He participated in the political life in Constantinople as a personal representative (*kapı kahyası*) of his brother Antioch Cantemir when his brother became the Prince of Moldavia.[41] He associated with many minorities and Ottoman dignitaries. He himself was appointed to the Moldavian principality in 1710. After his arrival in Moldavia, however, he joined forces with the Russians against the Ottomans and defected to Russia after the Russian defeat by the Ottomans in 1713.[42] He wrote his book on the history of the Ottoman Empire while he was in Russia.

In his book, Cantemir frequently refers to his life in Constantinople and especially to his palace. This palace was in the suburbs of Constantinople on a high hill called Sancakdar Yokuşu which had a view of almost the whole city and the suburbs.[43] Cantemir notes the two former owners of the lands on which he built his palace. One was Yusuf Efendi, son of the inspector of the navy, who sold the palace for "twenty-five hundred dolars[44] (sic)." Cantemir enlarged the palace with several buildings and ornaments. The former owner of some parts of the land was his father-in-law, Serban Cantacuzenus, Prince of Wallachia. Cantacuzenus had started building his palace under Mehmed III when he received an order to stop construction because his palace had become high enough to have a view of the interiors of the palace of *Tersane Sarayı*. Cantemir, by the intercession of the Grand Vezir Ali Paşa, obtained permission to extend his palace on these old foundations. Unfortunately, just as he had completed the construction, he was appointed to the principality of Moldavia and he left. He had subsequently heard that his palace was given to Sultan Ahmed's daughter who was also the wife of Ali Paşa the Grand Vezir.[45] This palace reflected the special status Cantemir had. Despite the housing restrictions, he was able to purchase land from an Ottoman dignitary and build a palace fit for the Sultan's daughter.

By the eighteenth century, all the Phanariots who lived in the district of Phanar seem to have distinguished themselves from the rest of the Ottoman minorities. Cantemir provides detailed description of the many intellectual activities among these Greeks, "the more noble and wealthy ones."[46] The district of Phanariot contained the patriarchal seat and the cathedral church as well as an academy built for the instruction of the youth. In this academy, philosophy in all its branches and other sciences were taught in old uncorrupted Greek. Most of Cantemir's and his sons' educators came from this academy. Cantemir learned the elements of philosophy from Jacomius, an accurate grammarian, and the precepts of philosophy from Jeremias Cacavela, Hieramonachus, and preacher of the great church in Constantinople. Anastasius Condoidi of the academy was the preceptor of his sons. Cantemir's portrayal of the Greek community of Phanariots was one of a closely knit interactive community that maintained its privileged position through academic training.

The relations Cantemir had with the Phanariots, other Ottoman minorities, and the Ottoman Moslems emerges in the discussion of a topic of general interest: music. The interest in music brought various segments of Ottoman society together through the mediation of an Ottoman minority with a special status, Cantemir. In describing his activities in music, Cantemir described the Ottoman scene of music:

> [There was] Kiemani Ahmed, a Renegade, and Angeli Orthodox, (both my teachers for fifteen years), and also Chelebico, a Jew, with the Turks, Darvish Othman, Curshunji ogli, his Scholar, Taschi ogli Sinek Mehemmed, and Bardakchi Mehemmed Chelebi, which two last, when they had been taught by one Camboso Mehemmed Aga, were afterwards with Ralaki Eupragiote a noble Greek of Constantinople, instructed by me in some parts of Musick, particularly in the Theory, and a new method of my own invention of expressing the Songs by Notes, unknown before to the Turks. I had also for Scholars in the Theory and Practice of Musick, Daul Ismail Effendi, first Treasurer of the Empire, and Latif Chelebi his Haznadar. By their request, I compos'd a little Book of the Art of Musick in Turkish, and dedicated it to the present Emperor.[47]

The teachers and students of Cantemir involved many people from among the Ottoman minorities and Ottoman dignitaries. This might have been a special circumstance due to the exceptional musical gifts of Cantemir. Even the possibility of such meetings for musical knowledge, however, reflects the extent of communication between some Ottoman minorities, Ottoman Moslems, and Ottoman dignitaries.

Cantemir's work also included very detailed accounts on the lives of various Ottoman vezirs such as Silahdar Hasan Paşa, Janissary ağas such as Çalık Ahmed, and governors such as Firari Hasan Paşa.[48] The personal nature of these accounts implies that Cantemir had close ties with Ottoman dignitaries, or with someone who had access to such information. Cantemir specifically described the Ottoman dignitaries he had personal relationships with. He knew "Cherkies Mehemmed Aga, Master of the imperial Stables, an intimate friend of mine,"[49] "the most learned Turk, Saadi Effendi (to whom alone I am indebted for my Turkish learning) . . . a great Mathematician and vers'd in the Democratean Philosophy."[50] He mentions another friend in greater detail.

> Haznader Ibrahim Pasha, at first treasurer to Cara Mustapha Pasha, then Beg of one of the gallies, afterwards ambassador extraordinary from the Othman court to the Emperor of Germany, and at last governor of Belgrade, with three horsetails. . . . Whilst I lived at Constantinople, I used often to invite him to my house, and did so gain his good will by treating him with wine, of which he was, though privately, an insatiable lover.[51]

The final portrait Cantemir provided of another friend, Nefioğlu Reis Efendi, is significant because of the great interest Nefioğlu had in the West. Unfortunately, there is no way of assessing the number of such Ottoman dignitaries interested in the West; the dignitary could be an exception and therefore carefully noted, or he could represent a general trend and be cited as a representative. Cantemir's portrayal can be studied with this reservation in mind.

> Under Husein Pasha, the promoter of peace of Carlowitz, there was . . . in the court of Mehemmed (IV), Reis Effendi, who was commonly called Nefi Ogly, or the Exile's son, because his father had been banished by Kioprili Ahmed Pasha. . . . I was intimately acquainted with him . . . and he certainly was the most learned man among the Turks, skilled not only in Arabic, and other aparts of learning in use among the Mahometans; but he also understood Latin, which he had learned by means of Meninskius's Turkish Grammar and Lexicon, without the assistance of a master . . . when any difficult matter occurred, it was customary for Rami (Pasha) to consult Nefiogly, and carry his opinion to the Vizir as his own.[52]

These portrayals reveal the diversity among the Ottoman dignitaries. Among them, some interacted and communicated with Cantemir and became receptive to the West.

These Ottoman minorities who had special status vis-à-vis the Ottoman state, unlike the minorities who acquired special status vis-à-vis the foreign embassies, faced fewer restrictions in their communication with Ottoman society. Their special official status helped them establish and cultivate social ties with Ottoman dignitaries and help transmit Western influence to the top echelons of Ottoman society. They were not able to establish ties with the rest of Ottoman society, however.

The perceptions this minority group had of the West must have been different from those of the Ottoman minorities. Because of their special status and special education, this group must have resisted total absorption by the West like their counterparts who entirely changed their style of life, dressing, and consumption habits. This special group must have absorbed Western knowledge rather than life styles. Because of this gradual absorption of Western knowledge, the Greek Phanariots must have slowly initiated Ottoman dignitaries into Western styles of thought.

Ottoman Dignitaries

The Ottoman dignitaries communicated with Ottoman minorities, foreign residents, and Ottoman ambassadors who had been to the West. Because of these exchanges, they were the first Moslem group to encounter the Western impact. The Ottoman dignitaries as a social group played the most crucial role of diffusing the Western impact into Ottoman society through their special position in that society.

The other groups of Ottoman society in Constantinople were the lower level officials, mostly Moslem, associated with the central Ottoman administration and the administration of Constantinople, those associated with religious foundations, Moslem tradesmen and artisans, a diverse group of laborers, and travelers from all parts of the Empire or the rest of the world. All these groups contributed to life in Constantinople, although none had the resources and communication opportunities available to the Ottoman dignitaries. Their lives were confined to their work and their immediate neighborhood. The economic, political, and social resources available to the Ottoman dignitaries enabled them extensive communication and mobility.[53]

There has been little research focusing on the position of the Ottoman dignitaries within Ottoman society. This section therefore explores the characteristics of the Ottoman dignitaries as a social group. It attempts to highlight their possible role in spreading the impact of the West to Ottoman society.

It is difficult to specify the members of the social group of Ottoman dignitaries. The most general definition[54] is based on their membership in the ruling military caste as *askeri,* distinct from the subject population of peasants and townspeople. This distinction becomes blurred because of the variation within the military; retired or unemployed *askeri*s, wives and children of *askeri*s, manumitted slaves of the Sultan and of the *askeri*s, and the families of the holders of religious public offices who attend the Sultan are also members of this caste. For these reasons, the term Ottoman dignitaries, a more encompassing term than Ottoman officials, a term implying occupational specifications, will be used.

Ottoman dignitaries were the high officials of the central administration, such as Grand Vezirs, vezirs, chiefs of the army and the navy, those in charge of the principal services in Constantinople, leading religious functionaries, and important members of the Palace.[55] The former Ottoman officials and leading families of the capital, who had exercised influence and who maintained their influence through the wealth and connections they had accumulated, are also included. Ottoman dignitaries were a diffuse group. Their only common quality derived from the economic, political, and social resources they controlled in the Ottoman society. This control was established through the ties they formed with each other, their households, and their vast wealth. The Ottoman dignitaries did not face any restrictions in communicating with either the minorities and foreign residents, or with the rest of Ottoman society. Their access to the rest of Ottoman society provided them with a crucial advantage over foreign residents and Ottoman minorities. They penetrated the Ottoman society through their vast households, properties, and endowments throughout the Empire.

During the Tulip Era, Ottoman dignitaries frequently interacted with each other in various shared interests. One such interest was raising tulips. Price registers of tulips from the years 1722–1727[56] contain entries of many high-priced tulips owned by Ottoman dignitaries. The Grand Admiral Mustafa Paşa registered forty-four kinds of tulips he himself had cross-bred. Damad İbrahim Paşa, his father-in-law, created six new types of tulips.[57] The Ottoman ambassador to Paris, Yirmisekiz Çelebi Mehmed Efendi, also registered some tulips.[58] The names of all these tulips reflected the Persian influence on contemporary Ottoman literature. Two of Mehmed Efendi's tulips, for example, were called *neyyir-i gülşen* (bright star of the garden), which was worth eighty *guruş* (where the highest listed tulip was worth two hundred), and *sagar-i sim* (bowl of silver), which was worth fifteen *guruş*. This interest in tulips induced interaction among the Ottoman dignitaries.

The interaction of the Ottoman dignitaries with the broader Ottoman society took place mainly through their households; the households were significant in the spread of the Western impact into Ottoman society. As there are no comparable social units today, a detailed description of Ottoman households is needed to depict its communication patterns with Ottoman society. The household will be studied in relation to its authority structure, residential pattern, members, and size.

The authority of the Ottoman dignitary over his household derived from and was sanctified by tradition. This authority helped the Ottoman dignitary shape his own household after his own image, in accordance with his own views. The household was influenced by and adhered to the master in all its relations; it played a vital role in absorbing and spreading the Western impact the master had received.

These large, extensive households shared a common residence. The common residence induced continuous communication, a common basis of loyalty and authority, and a solidarity in facing the rest of society. The residence was usually a large complex consisting of many kiosks, pavilions, coffee room, cellars, servants' quarters, privy, bakery, shed, arbor, stable, mill, fountains, well, pool, bath, and orchards.[59] The summer residences of the dignitaries were based on a similar pattern. Communication between household members all living in one residential unit must have intensified the authority and impact of the Ottoman dignitary on his household.

As it can be depicted from the residential pattern, the household of a dignitary formed a self-sufficient unit; it included a wide range of activities and members. Some household members were cooks, waiters, and their helpers for preparing food, personal grooms, tailors for clothing, carpenters, gardeners, architects for shelter, soldiers for security, the harem for reproduction, many teachers for education, poets, musicians for entertainment, physicians for maintaining health, an imam for religious functions within the household, carriage drivers, horse grooms for transportation, scribes and messengers for communication, and accountants and a treasurer for financial services. This extensive and diverse household incorporated people from all levels of Ottoman society.

The size of the households of Ottoman dignitaries increased especially after the seventeenth century when the Ottoman state stopped expanding. Ottoman volunteers could no longer take part in campaigns and receive land grants to improve their status. They started to attach themselves to the households of Ottoman dignitaries for chances of bettering their position in society, thereby entering into client relations with the dignitaries. With their incorporation, the household of the Ottoman dignitary consisted of his relatives, those raised and trained in the household, and those who later attached themselves to the household. The Ottoman dignitaries also acquired slaves for their households to be trained in the skills required by the household.[60] These slaves were either war captives or people brought most frequently from the Caucasus and sold by slave merchants at the slave market.

The Ottoman state initially supported the establishment of large households by the Ottoman dignitaries because of the services they provided to the Ottoman army in fighting during campaigns, and to the dignitary in fulfilling his duties during peace.[61] The retinue of a Grand Vezir, for example, consisted of at least two hundred members.[62] During the reign of Mehmed III (1595–1602), the Grand Vezir İbrahim Paşa had a household of five hundred members in addition to the nine hundred soldiers in his retinue. The household members increased even more during the seventeenth century. Grand Vezir Nasuh Paşa's household consisted of one thousand one members, the second vezir Mehmed Paşa of nine hundred, third vezir Gürcü Ahmed Paşa of five hundred, fourth vezir Davud Paşa of four hundred, fifth vezir Nakkaş Hasan Paşa of three hundred, sixth vezir Hadım Yusuf Paşa of three hundred, seventh vezir Halil Paşa of five hundred, and the secretary of financial affairs (*başdefterdar*) Ekmekçizade Ahmed Paşa of three hundred members.[63] These household sizes reveal the impact households must have had in Constantinople. Households of Ottoman dignitaries in the provinces were also comparable in size. In 1745, the governor of Adana Murtaza Paşa's household contained five hundred members, the governor of Sivas Selim Paşa's one thousand two hundred, governor of Trebizond Veli Paşa's eight hundred, the governor of Karaman Çelik Mehmed Paşa's one thousand, and the governor of Erzurum İbrahim Paşa's one thousand household members.[64]

These vast household sizes increased the amount of communication in Ottoman society. The relations between Ottoman dignitaries were emulated by the members of their respective households who also associated with each other socially. This communication between households intensified the associations of the dignitaries. Households also had frequent interaction with the rest of society in the marketplace, various shops and coffee houses, and in mosques. Marketplace communication included the minorities whereas that in the mosque was confined to Moslems. Through these exchanges, the household was able to gather and disseminate information. The Ottoman dignitary, as the master of this vast household, could disseminate his influence to the rest of Ottoman society through his household.

This household structure was patterned after the household of the Sultan.[65] It had an inner section where the palace pages served the Sultan's person; these pages trained for administrative positions in the outer section.[66] The pages educated in the palace school were originally Christian youths converted to Islam at an early age; after the abolition of this practice of conversion, Moslems and pages of the Ottoman dignitaries also joined this school.[67] Their education consisted of Turkish and Islamic culture, the reading of the Qur'an, lessons in Turkish, Arabic, and Persian, and training in sports and in arms. The pages were then assigned to positions considered commensurate with their skills.

Sons of the Sultan and some high-ranking Palace officials had their own retinues within the Palace.[68] These retinues provided the officials with the core of a household to be expanded when they were appointed to serve, mostly as governors, in the Ottoman provinces. The palace graduates were often given a wife, educated and trained in the harem, and a small retinue before they left the Palace as well.[69] By the seventeenth century, lowest level palace graduates started to join the households of the Ottoman officials directly. These connections helped pattern the households of the Ottoman dignitaries after that of the Sultan.

The very successful replication of the Sultan's household led Ottoman dignitaries to train large numbers of their household members. These people started to compete for Ottoman administrative appointments with those trained in the Palace. After the seventeenth century, more and more appointments to important positions in the provinces were made from among the household members of Ottoman dignitaries.[70] The influence of these dignitaries increased and spread into Ottoman society as members of their households were appointed to important administrative positions. The Western impact on the Ottoman dignitaries could thereby spread with them into the provinces.

As the households of Ottoman dignitaries increased in influence, more and more had to keep large households to maintain this influence. In these households, they would keep training their household members for administrative positions, and would benefit from the power obtained and the network that spread when their members acquired such positions. During the second half of the seventeenth century, most appointments for high offices in the central administration and the provinces were filled by men "who had been either raised, trained or attached to the households of Ottoman dignitaries."[71] Köprülü Mehmed Paşa, who was the grand vezir in 1656, had a very large household where he educated a sizable number of his pages in administrative skills. Thirty-eight of the forty-seven years following his ascendence in 1656 were dominated by Grand Vezirs of his household.[72]

The influence of the households of Ottoman dignitaries persisted in the eighteenth century. The recruitment of members for the households and their consequent influence on Ottoman society were reflected in Cantemir's accounts. There were frequent references to the fact that that some important Ottoman dignitaries were "brought up at the court of" another senior dignitary.[73] His account, in particular, of the Grand Vezir Çorlulu Ali Paşa portrayed one pattern of joining the household of an Ottoman dignitary and profiting from the opportunities it provided. The Paşa originally belonged to a poor family in Thrace and became a barber's apprentice to earn a living. His fortunes then changed:

> Cara Bairam ogli, a Capuji bashi, happens about that time to go from Constantinople to Adrianople . . . and lodges by the way at his [Ali's] father's house . . . observing the good countenance of the young man, he asks him whether he would follow him, and become an Othmanly, i.e. a courtier? The young man embraces the offer, but his parents are against it, on account, as they pretended, of their poverty. However, Ali goes even against their will with the Capuji bashi to Adrianople. Being put through school by him, he made such great progress in a short time, that Cara Bairam Ogly thought it more adviseable to bring him into the Sultan's palace, as a spacious theatre, in which his virtues might shine, and, by being his patron, enlarge one day his fortune, rather than keep him in his own house.[74]

The Ottoman dignitary could expand his influence by training members of his household himself or by sending them to the Sultan's household. The clientage system that developed over time helped the Ottoman dignitary to form a large network of relations through which he could exert his influence. The Ottoman dignitary interacted with Ottoman society in recruiting his household members. He also interacted with the Ottoman state by providing well-trained officials. This unique communication pattern enabled the Ottoman dignitary to spread his influence throughout Ottoman society. Once Western impact had reached the Ottoman dignitary, he had the networks and the resources to penetrate Ottoman society and spread the impact.

The economic resources of Ottoman dignitaries also facilitated their penetration into Ottoman society. Ottoman dignitaries owned properties in diverse parts of the Empire and used their households to maintain and regulate these properties. The religious endowment registers of Ottoman dignitaries provide abundant information on their properties.[75] In the eighteenth century, for example, the religious endowments of the Grand Vezir Damad İbrahim Paşa and the Grand Admiral Kaymak Mustafa Paşa detailed some of the properties owned by these two dignitaries throughout the Ottoman Empire.

The Grand Vezir endowed a complex of mosque, theological school, soup kitchen, school, library, bazaar, inn, and a public bath in his native village of Nevşehir.[76] To provide for the upkeep of this complex, İbrahim Paşa endowed income from some of his properties. These endowed properties were the village of Muşkara and its tributaries; in Constantinople, four large rented houses, a bazaar with twenty-seven shops, another with forty-nine; in Smyrna, eleven soap manufactories, one stone inn, six cellars, three slaughterhouses, two waxhouses, one coffeehouse, one bakery, one grocer, one sweet shop, one house where rooms were leased out to Jews (*Yahudhane*), one house where rooms were leased out to Europeans (*Frenghane*);[77] in Antioch, the half-share of thirteen mulberry gardens. All these scattered ownings required the household of the Grand Vezir to visit the properties, maintain them, and collect the revenues. The household had the opportunity to interact with some remote provinces of the Empire and spread the impact of their masters as they checked the properties.[78]

The other example[79] of such an endowment belonged to Grand Admiral Mustafa Paşa, the son-in-law of Damad İbrahim Paşa. To support the school and mosques he was building, Mustafa Paşa endowed the income accruing from some of his properties. These properties were, in Constantinople, a public bath, a stone room, a vegetable garden, two houses, a house with a grocer shop and a courtyard; in Smyrna, a house where rooms were leased out to Europeans,[80] two soap manufactories, two-thirds share of a public bath, another public bath, and the house of the bath-keeper; on the island of Lesbos, a field with six hundred olive trees, another field with olive trees; on the island of Chios, three dye-houses containing a room, a kitchen, and a courtyard, a tower with two rooms, one kitchen, three cellars, a well, and a garden with a pool, a vineyard, and a field. The properties in different regions of the Empire help explain the extent of penetration by an Ottoman dignitary.

Ottoman dignitaries were the pivotal group in the emergence of Western influence in Ottoman society. Through their interaction with the foreign residents in the Ottoman Empire, the Ottoman minorities, and Ottoman ambassadors to the West, the Ottoman dignitaries were affected by the rising Western powers and their impact. The Ottoman dignitaries were also able to communicate with the rest of Ottoman society, unlike the foreign residents and Ottoman minorities. Through their social, economic, and political positions, their vast households, and their properties in diverse Ottoman provinces, the Ottoman dignitaries could penetrate Ottoman society, and diffuse the Western impact into that society. The transformation of Ottoman society thus began.

9

Conclusion

One channel of Ottoman communication with the West, an Ottoman embassy, depicts the encounter between the Ottoman and French societies in the eighteenth century. The embassy of Yirmisekiz Çelebi Mehmed Efendi to France in 1720–1721 reveals the diversity between Ottoman and French societies. The social manners, entertainment patterns, aesthetic sensitivities, technological levels, and gift selections of the two societies differed. The Ottoman embassy in France sparked a brief fashion of Turquerie. The embassy signalled permanent changes in Ottoman society, however. Ottoman consumption habits were altered, new residences were built after the French model, and an Ottoman printing press was introduced. Mehmed Efendi's embassy reflected these changes for a number of reasons. It had been sent to observe France, the cultural center of the West, which was influencing all Western societies. Mehmed Efendi, as a learned man, had observed and apprehended the West and, on his return, had introduced its particularities to Ottoman society. As an Ottoman dignitary, Mehmed Efendi could influence Ottoman society more than men from other social groups who had relations with the West. Ottoman foreign residents were limited in their communications with the society at large by speaking a different language, professing a different faith, and living in special quarters under surveillance. Ottoman minorities still had difficulties in communication with Ottoman society due to differences in faith and restrictions in living quarters. Ottoman minorities also faced a linguistic barrier in the Ottoman period. Unlike the Arabic-speaking world, these minorities could not participate in Ottoman literary culture. They thereby lost another channel of communication with the rest of Ottoman society. Ottoman dignitaries had no such problems. With extensive households, properties throughout the empire, and positions near the Sultan, Ottoman dignitaries could spread their influence to the society at large. The West started to penetrate Ottoman society through their guidance.

The embassy and its reflections on Ottoman society help demonstrate the emerging Ottoman receptivity to the West. The pattern of changing Ottoman attitude toward the West can be compared to the experiences of other traditional societies with the West. Russian society encountered the West during the same period as the Ottoman society. Yet the Russian pattern of change was different from the Ottoman pattern. A comparison of Ottoman and Russian patterns can help illuminate additional elements in the gradual transformation of these traditional societies toward the West.

Other Ottoman sources can be used to show the response to the rise of the West. Ottoman trade registers, which specify Ottoman imports from the West, reveal the availability of Western goods to Ottoman society. Ottoman inheritance registers, which contain inventories of goods in the possession of the deceased, disclose the Ottoman ownership patterns of these Western goods. An analysis of these patterns throughout the eighteenth century can document rising Western influence in Ottoman society. Ottoman court cases on disputes over goods indicate the Ottoman usage of Western goods. Ottoman court records and inheritance registers exist for all sections of Ottoman society; the differences between Ottoman minorities, men and women, and regions of the Ottoman Empire can be studied from these records. These differences will help demonstrate the complexity of Western penetration into Ottoman society. Ottoman imperial orders pertaining to the relations with the West may further document the nature of the changing Ottoman relations with the West. All these sources will help reveal the process of Western penetration into a traditional society.

One important aspect in Western penetration and concomitant Ottoman transformation was the resistance within Ottoman society to this transformation. Ottoman social groups realigned themselves with regard to their views on Western penetration. Some resisted while others assisted. Hence, Ottoman society transformed itself in anticipation of the West. All these processes must be analyzed to understand how traditional societies change in response to the West.

APPENDIX A

THE TEXTS
OF MEHMED EFENDİ'S EMBASSY

There are twelve manuscripts of Mehmed Efendi's embassy. Of these manuscripts, four are in Turkey,[1] and six in various European countries.[2] A critical edition of all these manuscripts does not yet exist.

The seven printed editions of Mehmed Efendi's embassy were printed either in Constantinople or in Paris. Of the three editions printed in Constantinople, one, included in the historical chronicle *Tarih-i Raşid,* was printed in 1865,[3] the other in 1866,[4] while the last edition was printed in 1889.[5] The first French edition, which appeared in 1757,[6] was a translation of the account in *Tarih-i Raşid.* The other two French editions were printed in 1841 and 1889 in Ottoman to provide a textbook to French students learning Ottoman.[7] The last French edition, which came out recently in 1981, was based on the 1757 edition.[8]

One additional printed source contains an account of Mehmed Efendi's embassy.[9] Although the author of this work is not known, the copy in the Istanbul University Library[10] contains a handwritten note on the cover that "this work belongs to Lenoir, the dragoman (translator) of the French embassy, who accompanied the Ottoman ambassador to Paris in 1721." This account contains additional information on Mehmed Efendi's embassy, noting the exact dates of all of Mehmed Efendi's activities and describing in full detail the protocol observed in all his visits.

APPENDIX B

THE RETINUE
OF YİRMİSEKİZ ÇELEBİ MEHMED
EFENDİ

The retinue consisted of[1]

his personal secretary (his son, Mehmed Said)
an intendant
a Turkish *imam*
a treasurer, keeper of seals
master of robes
master of office
coffee maker
a pipe filler and maintainer
perfumer
laundryman
barber
candlestick filler and maintainer
thirteen ağas
master of ceremonies
steward
horsemen
chief cook
six kitchen aides
a physician[2] (Moise?) and his manservant
Solyman, a sea-captain ransomed by Mehmed Efendi on Malta
four tent guards
twenty footmen
water bearers
two men for the stable
two cloak men
one dressmaker
two valets
five caterers with two manservants
Lenoir, the Ottoman interpreter of the French embassy in Constantinople,
    with his sister and three valets
French engineer Lebon from Constantinople with a valet

APPENDIX C

THE ROUTE OF THE VOYAGE

7 October	1720	Departure from Constantinople
22 November	1720	Toulon (tulon)
22 November	1720 ⎫	Initial quarantine in Toulon
10 December	1720 ⎭	
16 December	1720	Montpellier (mompeliye)
17 December	1720 ⎫	Quarantine at Sète (set)
25 January	1721 ⎭	
25 January	1721 ⎫	Through the Languedoc (lankdok) Canal
1 February	1721 ⎭	
2 February	1721	Arrival at Toulouse (tuluz)
5 February	1721	Bordeaux (bordo)
15 February	1721	Havre de Grace (havr de gras)
8 March	1721	Arrival at Charenton (şiranton)
15 March	1721	Procession into Paris
21 March	1721	Reception by the king
12 July	1721	Audience with the king to leave
3 August	1721	Leaving Paris
27 August	1721	Lyon (lion)
6 September	1721	Arriving at Montpellier
7 September	1721	Embarking for Constantinople
8 October	1721	Arriving at Constantinople

Voyage by sea	46 days
Quarantine	39 days
Voyage by canal	21 days
Voyage by land	22 days
Stay in Paris	148 days
Voyage by land	24 days
Voyage by sea	31 days

Total voyage
7 October 1720–8 October 1721 (one year)

APPENDIX D

GIFT EXCHANGES

EMBASSY OF YİRMİSEKİZ ÇELEBİ MEHMED EFENDİ (1720–1721)

Gifts of Mehmed Efendi

To the King

two Arab horses harnessed with ermine fur
one arc with a quiver and sixty arrows
a saber encrusted with precious stones
two pieces of silk cloth from Greece and India
eight pieces of very fine muslin
an ermine fur coat
six bottles of Mecca balm

To the Regent

a richly harnessed horse
six pieces of brocade from Greece
four pieces of Indian cloth
an ermine coat
four handkerchiefs
six bottles of Mecca balm

To the Minister of Foreign Relations

an ermine fur coat

Gifts of the King

To Mehmed Efendi

a damaskin gun of gold
two pairs of gold pistols

one diamond studded belt for saber
two pieces of velvet with gold flowers
four carpets of la Savonnerie
two large mirrors by Colet
two commodes by Cresson
a nécessaire by Colet
two bureaus
a bookcase furnished with glass and a chest
,six clocks
six watches
six snuff boxes
other pieces of jewelry

To the Steward

a clock by Turret

To the Master of Ceremonies

a gold watch

To the Physician

a gold watch

EMBASSY OF MEHMED SAİD EFENDİ
(1741)

Gifts of Mehmed Said

To the King

one armor enriched with pearls
one velvet saddle enriched with diamonds
two gold and silver tissued straps
breast strap with a gold buckle
two stirrups enriched with diamonds
head stall with gold enameled diamonds
six sabers in silver with damask
one small velvet embroidered cushion
two gold pistols with precious stones
two pistols with fur covers

one cartridge pouch with diamonds
powder flask with diamonds
mace of rock crystal
two green velvet quivers with diamonds
four gilded silver guns
one gun with gold texture
one dagger with diamonds
one silver dagger with diamonds
one gold fiber enameled dagger
Indian dagger, silver engraved in relief
Indian dagger with a jade handle
Turkish knife with damask cover
Turkish knife with ivory handle

Gifts of the King

To Mehmed Said Efendi

silver chandeliers by Ballin
a round table for twelve persons
a hand-wash basin and a pitcher by Germain
two great mirrors
carpets of la Savonnerie
one great organ
furniture with inlaid work
a microscope by M. Lebas, etc.

APPENDIX E

THE HOUSEHOLD OF THE GRAND VEZIR

The household of a vezir could be grouped into five sections.[1] The first consisted of the officials attached to the office of the Grand Vezir such as the assistant to the vezir (*kethüda-ı sadr-ı âli*), secretary of foreign affairs (*reisülküttab*), chief of the guards (*çavuşbaşı*), official memoranda writers (*tezkireciler*), chief secretary (*mektupçu*), chief of correspondence (*amedçi*), master of ceremonies (*teşrifatçı*), official in charge of the stationery (*divitdar*), official making report summaries for the sultan (*telhisci*), and others.

The second section contained the vezir's personal retinue. It was divided into the inner (*enderun*) and outer (*birun*) sections which were headed by two sets of ağas. The ağas of the inner section *enderun* (also called inner ağas (*iç ağaları*), or bearded ağas (*sakallı ağalar*)) consisted of the imam, keeper of the wardrobe (*kaftani*) and his retinue, ağa in charge of table napkins (*peşkir ağası*) and his retinue, ağa in charge of the candlesticks (*şamdan ağası*) and his retinue, ağa in charge of paste and taffy (*macun ağası*) and his retinue, head towel-keeper (*makramebaşı*) and his retinue, head in charge of prayer rugs (*seccadecibaşı*) and his retinue, superintendent of ablutions (*ibriktar ağa*) and his retinue, head-keeper of tobacco (*duhancıbaşı*) and his retinue, head of ammunition (*cephanecibaşı*) and his retinue, head butler (*sofracıbaşı*) and his retinue, the treasurer ağa (*hazinedarbaşı*) and his retinue, his assistant, head of horse-men (*cündibaşı*) and his retinue, head muezzin and his retinue, head guard of the *enderun* section (*enderun başçavuşu*), person in charge of stationery (*divitdar*), guards, mutes, the military band (*mehteran-ı enderun*), ağa of the spears and lances (*mızrakçı ağa*) and others.

The ağas of the outer section *birun* (also called outer ağas (*dış ağalar*) or ağas with moustaches (*bıyıklı ağalar*) or regular ağas (*gedikli ağalar*)) consisted of the sword-bearer ağa (*silahdar ağa*), ağa of the footmen (*çuhadar ağa*), master of ceremonies (*selam ağası*), head-keeper of locks (*miftah ağası*), head-keeper of seals (*sermühürdar*), head-keeper of turbans (*destar ağası*), chief of door-keepers (*kapıcılar kethüdası*), ağa of the stables (*mirahur ağa*), ağa of the pantry (*kiler ağası*), ağa of censers (*buhurdan ağası*), head of irregular cavalry (*delilbaşı*), head of messengers (*kavasbaşı*), head-keeper of fur coats (*kürkçübaşı*), head of saddlers (*saraçbaşı*), keeper of rifleguards (*tüfekçibaşı*), ağa of the first regiment of the Ottoman household cavalry (*baş silahşör ağa*), head-coffee maker (*kahvecibaşı*), head-keeper of linen (*çamaşırcıbaşı*), gatekeepers (*bevvabin*), and others.

The third section consisted of the assistants of previous section members ranging in number from ninety to two hundred depending on the wealth of the specific dignitary. It also included the cooks (*aşçı*), persons who go to the market (*pazarcı*), and stewards (*vekilharç*).

The fourth section included those members whose functions were required in transportation and in campaigns. They consisted of quarter-masters (*müteferrika*), ağas used in communication (*tebdil ağası*), chief of tent-pitchers (*çadır mehterbaşısı*), head of packsaddles (*semercibaşı*), assistant of the stables (*ahur kethüdası*), head of the camel keepers (*sarbanbaşı*), bearers of horse-tails (*tuğcu*), persons in charge of spare horses (*yedekçi*), sergeants at arms (*alay çavuşları*), keepers of hounds (*sadrazam segbanları*), flask-bearers (*matracı*), rifle bearer (*tüfenkçi*), guide (*deli*), messenger (*peyk*), guardsman in attendance (*solak*), running attendant (*satır*), standard-bearer (*sancakdar*), person in charge of boats (*filikacı*), halberdier (*harbeci*), tatars (*tatar*) used in communication, blacksmith (*nalband*), grooms (*seyis*), tent-pitcher and baggage muleteer (*akkam*), water-carriers with mules (*katırcı sakalar*), and others.

The fifth section consisted of the eunuchs who presided over the harem of the Grand Vezir.

NOTES

Introduction

1. This process is discussed in detail by Braudel in *The Wheels of Commerce* (New York 1982 edition) and by Mumford in *The Culture of Cities* (New York 1938).

2. The document was edited by Unat in ''Ahmet III. Devri,'' pp. 107–121. Lewis, *Emergence,* p. 45; Berkes, *Development,* p. 30; Akıncı, *Türk-Fransız,* p. 45 use this document.

3. Uzunçarşılı, *Osmanlı Tarihi,* p. 47.

4. Itzkowitz, *Mübadele,* p. 4.

5. Berkes, *Development,* p. 33; Lewis, *Emergence,* pp. 45–46; Lewis, *Muslim Discovery,* p. 240.

6. Karal, in *Tanzimat,* p. 8.

Chapter 1

1. *Tarih-i Raşid,* vol. V, pp. 213–214.

2. The War of Spanish Succession between France, England, and Austria lasted from 1701 to 1714. The Great Northern War between Sweden, helped by England and Holland, against Russia, Denmark, and Poland lasted from 1700 to 1721.

3. Shaw, *History,* vol. I, pp. 217–240.

4. Akıncı, *Türk-Fransız,* p. 13; Lemontey, *Histoire,* p. 445.

5. Berkes, *Development,* p. 25.

6. Vitol, ''From the History,'' p. 126.

7. Martin, *Histoire,* p. 103; Lemontey, *Histoire,* p. 445.

8. Louis XV appointed Chevalier de Camilly as the commander of the vessels taking Mehmed Efendi back to Constantinople. Camilly's detailed account of this mission has been edited by Armand Gasté, ''Retour à Constantinople de l'Ambassadeur Turc Méhémet Effendi: Journal de Bord du Chevalier de Camilly, Juillet 1721– Mai 1722.'' The quotation is on pp. 100–101.

9. Lemontey, *Histoire,* p. 449; Martin, *Histoire,* p. 104.

10. Ahmed Refik, *Lale Devri,* p. 45.

11. The chain of command consisted of the grand vezir, sheik ul islam, the secretary of finance, the secretary in charge of foreign affairs, and grand admiral. The

Ottoman terms are *vezir-i azam, şeyhülislam, başdefterdar, reisülküttab, kaptan-ı derya*.

12. Uzunçarşılı, *Osmanlı Tarihi*, pp. 148, 167.

13. The Ottoman term is *kethüda-ı sadr-ı ali*.

14. Some examples of these clichés are "iftihar ül ümera il üzzam il iseviye muhtar ül kübera il f'il millet il mesihiye" and "sahib-i ezyal ül haşmet v'el vekar sahib-i delail ul mecd v'el itibar muslih-i mesalih-i cemahir ül taifet il nasraniye."

15. Uzunçarşılı, *Osmanlı Tarihi*, pp. 170–171.

16. For example, Tunaya, *Türkiye'nin*, pp. 20–21; Karal, in *Tanzimat*, p. 7; Berkes, *Development*, pp. 25–27.

17. Unat, *Osmanlı Sefirleri*, pp. 17–19.

18. Among those envoys whose names are known, one is an *ağa*, two are men trained in the Palace *müteferrikas*, and one is a herald *çavuş*. See *Le Paradis*, pp. 22–23.

19. d'Aubigny, "Un Ambassadeur," p. 83; Desmet-Grégoire, *Divan Magique*, pp. 18–19.

20. The Ottoman terms for these posts are *sultan, sadrazam, reisülküttab, tercümanbaşı*.

21. The Ottoman expression is "*tertib-i muhaverat ve desayis-i nasaraya ittila hasıl etmiş*," *Tarih-i Raşid*, pp. 213–214. Unat also uses this quotation in *Osmanlı Sefirleri*, pp. 23–24.

22. Lewis, *Muslim Discovery*, p. 114; *Le Paradis*, pp. 24, 28.

23. The *Porte* was a term used by the Ottomans and foreigners to refer to the Ottoman state in general, or the Ottoman central administration in Constantinople in particular. The most frequently used Ottoman term for the same word is *Bab-ı Âli*.

24. Schefer, *Mémoire*, p. xlii.

25. Schefer, *Mémoire*, p. xliii; Unat, *Osmanlı Sefirleri*, p. 53; Ahmed Refik, *Tarihi*, p. 21.

26. Schefer, *Mémoire*, p. xliii; Unat, *Osmanlı Sefirleri*, pp. 53–54; Ahmed Refik, *Tarihi*, p. 21.

27. *Le Paradis*, pp. 28–30.

28. d'Aubigny, "Un Ambassadeur," p. 81; see figure on page 11 for a drawing of Yirmisekiz Çelebi Mehmed Efendi.

29. Mehmed Süreyya, *Sicil*, vol. 4, p. 226; *Mufassal*, vol. 5, p. 2441; Danışmend, *İzahlı*, vol. 4, p. 481.

30. Schefer, *Mémoire*, p. xliii.

31. Gasté, "Retour," pp. 93–95.

32. Ibid., p. 90.

33. *Sefaretname-i Fransa*, p. 130; *Mehmed Efendi'nin Sefaretnamesi*, pp. 23–24; *Le Paradis*, p. 90.

34. Ahmed Refik, "Pasarofça Muahedesinden sonra Viyana'ya Sefir İ'zamı," *Tarih-i Osmani Encümeni Mecmuası* (hereafter *TOEM*), VII(1915), pp. 211–227.

35. Ibid., pp. 224–225.

36. Ibid., p. 221.

37. Itzkowitz, *Mübadele,* p. 23.

38. Unat, *Osmanlı Sefirleri,* pp. 25, 31–32.

39. See Appendix B for a detailed description of his retinue.

40. Pakalın, *Osmanlı Tarih,* p. 138.

41. E. Kuran, *Avrupa'da İkamet Elçiliklerinin,* p. 9.

42. See *Evliya Çelebi Seyahatnamesi,* Istanbul, vol. 7, pp. 146–205. There is a German translation by R. F. Kreutel, *Im Reiche des Goldenen Apfels,* Graz 1957.

43. Such as that presented by A. I. Hoci in *TOEM,* I(1911), p. 659.

44. The term frequently used is *tarafımızca malum oldukta.*

45. "Defter-i müsevvedat-i in'am ve tasaddukat ve teşrifat ve irsaliyat ve 'adet ve nukeriye ve gayrihu vacib-i sene tıs'a ve tıs'a mie" in Ö. L. Barkan's article "Istanbul Saraylarına ait Muhasebe Defterleri."

46. d'Aubigny, "Un Ambassadeur," p. 83.

47. Ahmed Refik, "Sultan Ahmed Salis ve Damadı," p. 150.

48. Ahmed Refik, "Sultan Ahmed Salisin Hayatına dair," pp. 229–232.

49. Unat, *Osmanlı Sefirleri,* p. 57; this manuscript is catalogued in Köprülü Library under No. 202 in a volume containing three other treatises. Unat also mentions two manuscripts under Nos. 2062 and 2063 in the Esad Efendi manuscript section of the library. These two manuscripts, compiled in 1725 by unknown authors, are titled *A Summary of the Condition of Europe.* Unat hypothesizes that these manuscripts are an addendum to Mehmed Efendi's embassy account. He provides two related facts to support his hypothesis: The manuscript mentions that the information contained was provided by a monk in Toulouse. There are no known Ottoman travelers to that region during this period except Mehmed Efendi and his retinue.

50. See Appendix A for a discussion of these texts.

51. 1757 edition.

52. Located in Bibliothèque Nationale, Ms. frç. 10777.

53. Located in Archives des Affaires Etrangeres, M. et D., X, 21.

54. The manuscript belongs to Şevket Rado who edited and published the book *Yirmisekiz Mehmed Çelebi'nin Fransa Seyahatnamesi,* abridged edition, Istanbul, 1970. In pp. 17–19, Rado provides some information on the manuscript.

55. *Le Paradis,* pp. 57, 171.

56. *Le Paradis,* p. 58; *Mehmed Efendi'nin Sefaretnamesi,* p. 1; *Sefaretname-i Fransa,* p. 109.

57. *Le Paradis,* p. 69; *Sefaretname-i Fransa,* p. 115; *Mehmed Efendi'nin Sefaretnamesi,* p. 8.

58. *Le Paradis,* G. Veinstein, ed., p. 102; *Sefaretname-i Fransa* 137; *Mehmed Efendi'nin Sefaretnamesi,* p. 21.

59. For the Persian verses, see *Le Paradis,* pp. 59, 159; *Sefaretname-i Fransa,* pp. 110, 173; *Mehmed Efendi'nin Sefaretnamesi,* pp. 2, 76.

60. *Le Paradis,* p. 126; *Sefaretname-i Fransa,* p. 154; *Mehmed Efendi'nin Sefaretnamesi,* p. 51. The phrase he used was *eddünya sicnül-mümin ve cennet-ül-kafir.* The *Mercure* of June and July 1721, part II, p. 96, and *Nouvelle Description,* p. 253, mention Mehmed Efendi's trip to Marly.

61. See Appendix C for the route of the voyage; the Ottoman spellings of the French words are also provided. The figure on page 19 contains a map of Mehmed Efendi's itinerary.

62. Desmet-Grégoire, *Divan Magique*, p. 20.

63. *Le Paradis*, p. 84; *Sefaretname-i Fransa*, p. 126; *Mehmed Efendi'nin Sefaretnamesi*, p. 19.

64. *Sefaretname: 1205 senesinde Prusya Kralı İkinci Frederik Giyomun nezdine memur olan Ahmed Azmi Efendinindir*, Konstantiniye 1303.

65. Lewis, *Muslim Discovery*, pp. 128–129.

66. d'Ohsson, *Tableau*, p. 391.

67. *Le Paradis*, pp. 63–69; *Sefaretname-i Fransa*, pp. 113–116; *Mehmed Efendi'nin Sefaretnamesi*, p. 5.

68. *Le Paradis*, pp. 63–64; *Sefaretname-i Fransa*, p. 112; *Mehmed Efendi'nin Sefaretnamesi*, p. 4.

69. *Sefaretname-i Fransa*, p. 115. Note that the French versions, *Le Paradis*, p. 69; *Histoire de la Ville*, p. 311, are different where they initially describe Sète as containing the place of quarantine. This is not how Mehmed Efendi perceived it.

70. d'Aubigny, "Un Ambassadeur," p. 85.

71. Ibid., p. 80.

72. Ibid., p. 85.

73. d'Ohsson, *Tableau*, p. 407.

74. *Le Paradis*, p. 67; *Sefaretname-i Fransa*, pp. 114–115; *Mehmed Efendi'nin Sefaretnamesi*, p. 6.

75. *Le Paradis*, p. 67.

76. *Le Paradis*, p. 74; *Sefaretname-i Fransa*, pp. 118–119; *Mehmed Efendi'nin Sefaretnamesi*, p. 11.

77. *Le Paradis*, pp. 79–80; *Sefaretname-i Fransa*, pp. 122–123; *Mehmed Efendi'nin Sefaretnamesi*, pp. 15–16.

Chapter 2

1. *Le Paradis*, p. 126; *Sefaretname-i Fransa*, p. 154; *Mehmed Efendi'nin Sefaretnamesi*, p. 51. As cited earlier, this quotation is not originally from the Qur'an.

2. Wortley Montagu, Lady Mary, *Complete Letters*, pp. 414–415.

3. The secrets of the draught were discovered and the chimney construction altered as a result of an advance in "caminology." Braudel, *The Structures*, p. 299.

4. All these developments are discussed by Braudel throughout *The Structures of Everyday Life*.

5. *Sefaretname-i Fransa*, pp. 153–155; *Mehmed Efendi'nin Sefaretnamesi*, pp. 49–51; *Le Paradis*, pp. 124–127.

6. Braudel cites this particular example in *The Structures*, p. 206.

7. *Sefaretname-i Fransa*, p. 122; *Mehmed Efendi'nin Sefaretnamesi*, p. 15; *Le Paradis*, p. 79.

8. *Sefaretname-i Fransa*, p. 155; *Mehmed Efendi'nin Sefaretnamesi*, p. 51; *Le Paradis*, p. 128.

9. *Sefaretname-i Fransa*, p. 160; *Mehmed Efendi'nin Sefaretnamesi*, p. 58; *Le Paradis*, p. 135.

10. *Sefaretname-i Fransa*, pp. 109, 117; *Mehmed Efendi'nin Sefaretnamesi*, pp. 1, 9; *Le Paradis*, pp. 58, 72.

11. *Sefaretname-i Fransa*, pp. 113, 117; *Mehmed Efendi'nin Sefaretnamesi*, pp. 5, 9; *Le Paradis*, pp. 64, 72.

12. *Sefaretname-i Fransa*, pp. 113, 118; *Mehmed Efendi'nin Sefaretnamesi*, pp. 5, 10; *Le Paradis*, pp. 65, 72.

13. *Sefaretname-i Fransa*, p. 125; *Mehmed Efendi'nin Sefaretnamesi*, p. 19; *Le Paradis*, p. 83.

14. *Sefaretname-i Fransa*, p. 130; *Mehmed Efendi'nin Sefaretnamesi*, p. 24; *Le Paradis*, p. 90.

15. *Sefaretname-i Fransa*, p. 148; *Mehmed Efendi'nin Sefaretnamesi*, p. 44; *Le Paradis*, p. 118.

16. *Sefaretname-i Fransa*, p. 112; *Mehmed Efendi'nin Sefaretnamesi*, p. 5; *Le Paradis*, p. 64.

17. *Sefaretname-i Fransa*, pp. 130, 136, 139; *Mehmed Efendi'nin Sefaretnamesi*, pp. 24, 30, 34; *Le Paradis*, pp. 90, 100, 106.

18. *Sefaretname-i Fransa*, p. 116; *Mehmed Efendi'nin Sefaretnamesi*, p. 9; *Le Paradis*, p. 71.

19. *Sefaretname-i Fransa*, p. 132; *Mehmed Efendi'nin Sefaretnamesi*, p. 6; *Le Paradis*, p. 94.

20. *Sefaretname-i Fransa*, p. 114; *Mehmed Efendi'nin Sefaretnamesi*, p. 6; *Le Paradis*, p. 67.

21. *Sefaretname-i Fransa*, pp. 126, 133–134; *Mehmed Efendi'nin Sefaretnamesi*, pp. 20, 28; *Le Paradis*, p. 85.

22. *Sefaretname-i Fransa*, p. 171; *Mehmed Efendi'nin Sefaretnamesi*, pp. 69–70; *Le Paradis*, p. 156.

23. *Sefaretname-i Fransa*, p. 149; *Mehmed Efendi'nin Sefaretnamesi*, p. 45; *Le Paradis*, p. 119.

24. *Sefaretname-i Fransa*, p. 134; *Mehmed Efendi'nin Sefaretnamesi*, p. 28.

25. *Sefaretname-i Fransa*, p. 135; *Mehmed Efendi'nin Sefaretnamesi*, pp. 29–30; *Le Paradis*, p. 99.

26. *Sefaretname-i Fransa*, p. 129; *Mehmed Efendi'nin Sefaretnamesi*, p. 23; *Le Paradis*, p. 89.

27. *Sefaretname-i Fransa*, pp. 139–140; *Mehmed Efendi'nin Sefaretnamesi*, p. 35; *Le Paradis*, pp. 106–107.

28. *Sefaretname-i Fransa*, p. 175; *Mehmed Efendi'nin Sefaretnamesi*, p. 74; *Le Paradis*, p. 162.

29. *Sefaretname-i Fransa*, p. 134; *Mehmed Efendi'nin Sefaretnamesi*, p. 28.

30. *Sefaretname-i Fransa*, p. 127; *Mehmed Efendi'nin Sefaretnamesi*, pp. 20–21; *Le Paradis*, p. 86.

31. *Sefaretname-i Fransa*, p. 128; *Mehmed Efendi'nin Sefaretnamesi*, p. 21; *Le Paradis*, p. 87.

32. *Sefaretname-i Fransa*, p. 149; *Mehmed Efendi'nin Sefaretnamesi*, p. 45; *Le Paradis*, p. 120.

33. *Sefaretname-i Fransa*, p. 149; *Mehmed Efendi'nin Sefaretnamesi*, p. 28.

34. *Sefaretname-i Fransa*, p. 134; *Mehmed Efendi'nin Sefaretnamesi*, p. 28.

35. *Sefaretname-i Fransa*, p. 139; *Mehmed Efendi'nin Sefaretnamesi*, p. 34; *Le Paradis*, pp. 105–106.

36. *Sefaretname-i Fransa*, p. 123; *Mehmed Efendi'nin Sefaretnamesi*, p. 16; *Le Paradis*, p. 80.

37. *Sefaretname-i Fransa*, p. 145; *Mehmed Efendi'nin Sefaretnamesi*, pp. 40–41; *Le Paradis*, pp. 113–114. Veinstein (*Le Paradis*) states thirteen as the legal age of puberty in France; Louis XV was coronated in October 1722.

38. *Sefaretname-i Fransa*, p. 138; *Mehmed Efendi'nin Sefaretnamesi*, pp. 32–33; *Le Paradis*, p. 104.

39. *Sefaretname-i Fransa*, p. 137; *Mehmed Efendi'nin Sefaretnamesi*, p. 32; *Le Paradis*, p. 103.

40. The position of a minister was created in the Ottoman state about a century later.

41. *Sefaretname-i Fransa*, p. 141; *Mehmed Efendi'nin Sefaretnamesi*, p. 37; *Le Paradis*, p. 109.

42. *Sefaretname-i Fransa*, p. 163; *Mehmed Efendi'nin Sefaretnamesi*, p. 60; *Le Paradis*, p. 139.

43. *Sefaretname-i Fransa*, p. 137; *Mehmed Efendi'nin Sefaretnamesi*, p. 32; *Le Paradis*, pp. 102–103.

44. *Sefaretname-i Fransa*, p. 176; *Mehmed Efendi'nin Sefaretnamesi*, pp. 75–76; *Le Paradis*, p. 164. The Ottoman term Mehmed Efendi uses is *papas-ı nasıpas*.

45. The term Mehmed Efendi uses is *hakim-i müstakil*.

46. *Sefaretname-i Fransa*, p. 121; *Mehmed Efendi'nin Sefaretnamesi*, p. 14; *Le Paradis*, p. 77.

47. *Sefaretname-i Fransa*, pp. 122–123; *Mehmed Efendi'nin Sefaretnamesi*, pp. 15–16, *Le Paradis*, pp. 79–80.

48. The original Ottoman term he uses is *serbest şehir*. The word *serbest*, borrowed from Persian, means free, independent; it emphasizes the absence of state control.

49. The Ottoman term *imtiyazlı şehir*, "privileged city," might have been more appropriate.

50. Herbette, *Une Ambassade*, p. 6.

51. Ibid., pp. 59, 109, 285.

52. d'Aubigny, "Un Ambassadeur," p. 80.

53. Spirodonakis, *Empire Ottoman*, p. 45.

54. d'Aubigny, "Un Ambassadeur," p. 91; *Le Mercure* of March 1721, pp. 126–132. Mehmed Efendi entered the city on 16 March 1721 as large crowds gathered to watch. King Louis XV was watching Mehmed Efendi's entrance incognito at Madame la Maréchale de Boussler's residence.

55. Gasté, "Journal de Bord," p. 95.

56. See figures on pages 32 and 33 for two such engravings.

57. Orgun, "Osmanlı Imparatorluğunda," pp. 407–408; d'Ohsson, *Le Tableau*, pp. 488–501.

58. Buvat, *Journal*, pp. 225–228, *Gazette de France* put out a special issue on the entrance of Mehmed Efendi to Paris and his audience with the King, No. 15, 30 March 1721.

59. *Nouvelle Description*, pp. 241–242.

60. See figures on pages 35 and 36.

61. Braudel, *The Structures*, p. 332.

62. d'Ohsson, *Le Tableau*, p. 30.

63. Le Dran account in *Le Paradis*, p. 230.

64. For the Ottoman eating habits see d'Ohsson, *Le Tableau*, pp. 30–36; Le Dran account in *Le Paradis*, p. 230.

65. See figures on pages 39 and 40.

66. Braudel, *The Structures*, pp. 183, 187, 206. The account above summarizes these pages.

67. *Le Paradis*, p. 94; *Sefaretname-i Fransa*, pp. 132–133; *Mehmed Efendi'nin Sefaretnamesi*, pp. 26–27.

68. Norbert Elias explains the complicated ceremony attached every morning to the King's getting up from sleep and every evening his going to sleep. *The Court Society*, pp. 83–89.

69. *Sefaretname-i Fransa*, p. 143; *Mehmed Efendi'nin Sefaretnamesi*, p. 38; *Le Paradis*, pp. 111–112.

70. *Sefaretname-i Fransa*, p. 144; *Mehmed Efendi'nin Sefaretnamesi*, pp. 38–39; *Le Paradis*, p. 112.

71. *Sefaretname-i Fransa*, pp. 148–149; *Mehmed Efendi'nin Sefaretnamesi*, pp. 44–45; *Le Paradis*, pp. 118–119.

72. Buvat, *Journal*, pp. 250–251; *Le Mercure*, of May 1721, p. 144.

73. d'Aubigny, "Un Ambassadeur," p. 86; Le Dran account in *Le Paradis*, p. 230; Saint-Simon, *Mémoires*, p. 202.

74. Braudel, *The Structures*, p. 234.

75. d'Ohsson, *Le Tableau*, p. 48.

76. Wortley Montagu, Lady Mary, *Complete Letters*, p. 318.

77. d'Aubigny, "Un Ambassadeur," p. 86; Le Dran account in *Le Paradis*, p. 229.

78. Buvat, *Journal*, pp. 244–245.

79. Ibid., p. 233.

80. d'Aubigny, "Un Ambassadeur," pp. 233–235.

81. Marais, *Journal et Mémoires*, p. 118.

82. Ahmet Azmi, *Sefaretname*, pp. 42–43.

83. Lewis, *Muslim Discovery*, p. 299.

84. *Le Paradis*, pp. 76, 85; *Sefaretname-i Fransa*, pp. 120, 126–127; *Mehmed Efendi'nin Sefaretnamesi*, pp. 20–21.

85. For the case of a Moroccan ambassador's similar view of Spanish women, see Henri Pérès *L'Espagne vue par les Voyageurs Musulmans*, p. 32.

86. Evliya Çelebi, *Seyahatname,* p. 200.

87. *Le Paradis,* pp. 73–74; *Sefaretname-i Fransa,* p. 118; *Mehmed Efendi' nin Sefaretnamesi,* p. 11.

88. *Le Paradis,* p. 135; *Mehmed Efendi' nin Sefaretnamesi,* p. 25; *Sefaretname-i Fransa,* p. 160.

89. d'Aubigny, "Un Ambassadeur," p. 88; *Nouvelle Description,* p. 221.

90. Saint-Simon, *Mémoires,* p. 202.

91. Buvat, *Journal,* p. 225.

92. d'Aubigny, "Un Ambassadeur," p. 209.

93. Buvat, *Journal,* p. 218. The lady was now married to Marquis de Cannilac, Lieutenant Captain of the Black Musketeers. *Le Mercure* of May 1721, p. 140.

94. For popular entertainment in the Ottoman Empire, see And, *History of,* pp. 17, 18, 23.

95. And, *A History of Theatre and Popular Entertainment in Turkey.*

96. See figures on pages 48 and 49.

97. Herbette, *Une Ambassade Persane,* pp. 50–51.

98. Buvat, *Journal,* p. 229.

99. Mehmed Efendi then went to the opera a second time to see *La Tragédie d'Omphale,* words by La Mothe, music by Destouches. His son later saw the ballet entitled *Les Fêtes Venitiennes. Le Paradis,* p. 117; *Le Mercure* of March 1721, pp. 169–170; *Nouvelle Description,* p. 249.

100. *Le Paradis,* pp. 115–118; *Sefaretname-i Fransa,* pp. 146–148; *Mehmed Efendi' nin Sefaretnamesi,* pp. 41–43.

101. *Le Paradis,* pp. 118–119; *Sefaretname-i Fransa,* pp. 148–149; *Mehmed Efendi' nin Sefaretnamesi,* p. 45. This "event" was presented in the Salle de Machines at the Louvre. *Le Mercure* of May 1721, p. 140.

102. The performance he attended was a comedy of Scaron called *Dom Japhet d'Arménie* which had been reduced to three acts with intermissions, songs, and dances. *Mercure* of June and July 1721, part I, p. 133.

103. Ahmed Azmi, *Sefaretname,* p. 38.

104. For example, the concert from the symphonies of M. de Lully mentioned in *Mercure* of April 1721, p. 174; Buvat, *Journal,* p. 239.

105. For this account, see Buvat, *Journal,* pp. 258–259; Marais, *Journal et Mémoires,* p. 162; *Mercure* of June and July 1721, part II, p. 4, states that the French Royal Academy of Music "gave a concert on Turkish verses."

106. *Sefaretname-i Fransa,* p. 143.

107. d'Aubigny, "Un Ambassadeur," p. 207.

108. Balleroy, *Les Correspondants,* pp. 311–312; *Le Mercure* of April 1721, pp. 166–167. Mehmed Efendi presented the Abbot Bignon the Royal Librarian, with whom he held the discourse on music, with a Greek liturgy and two Armenian liturgies.

109. Ahmed Azmi, *Sefaretname,* p. 38.

110. Elias, *The Court Society,* p. 79. Social life then spread from the residences of

court members to those of the financiers, eventually producing the "salon culture."
Elias interprets this shift as a slow decentralization of court life.

111. *Sefaretname-i Fransa*, p. 173; *Mehmed Efendi'nin Sefaretnamesi*, pp. 72–73;
Le Paradis, pp. 159–160.

112. See figures on pages 52 and 53.

113. d'Ohsson, *Le Tableau*, p. 241.

114. These late hours resulted from the new French meal hours. Braudel states that
in the eighteenth century, "the Parisians dined at two o'clock and the nobles at three in
the afternoon. Supper was taken at nine in Paris while the nobles supped at ten at
night." Braudel, *The Structures*, p. 328.

115. Buvat, *Journal*, pp. 258–259; *Mercure de France*, p. 196.

116. All these generalizations apply only to the upper classes and may not be
generalized to the populace. The upper classes dominate the observations since they
were the ones who defined the culture.

117. *Le Paradis*, pp. 104–105; *Sefaretname-i Fransa*, p. 138; *Mehmed Efendi'nin
Sefaretnamesi*, p. 33.

118. *Le Paradis*, pp. 155–157; *Sefaretname-i Fransa*, pp. 170–171; *Mehmed
Efendi'nin Sefaretnamesi*, pp. 26–29.

119. Wortley Montagu, Lady Mary, *Complete Letters*, pp. 342–343.

120. d'Ohsson, *Le Tableau*, pp. 233–234.

121. Wortley Montagu, Lady Mary, *Complete Letters*, p. 414.

122. Ibid., p. 414.

123. See d'Ohsson, *Le Tableau*, pp. 170–176, and Braudel, *The Structures*, pp.
286–290, for detailed descriptions.

124. Gaste, "Retour," pp. 94–95.

125. *Le Paradis*, p. 135; *Sefaretname-i Fransa*, p. 160.

126. *La Grande Larousse* has an estimate of 500,000 while Braudel in *The Structures* p. 526, quotes an estimate of 400,000.

127. H. İnalcık, "Istanbul" article in the *Encyclopedia of Islam*, p. 244.

128. Braudel, *The Structures*, p. 507.

129. Ibid., p. 268.

130. *Le Paradis*, p. 88; *Sefaretname-i Fransa*, p. 128; *Mehmed Efendi'nin Sefaretnamesi*, p. 24.

131. The term is *bedi ül üslup*. *Le Paradis*, p. 89; *Sefaretname-i Fransa*, p. 129;
Mehmed Efendi'nin Sefaretnamesi, p. 25.

132. *Le Paradis*, pp. 157–158; *Sefaretname-i Fransa*, pp. 171–172; *Mehmed
Efendi'nin Sefaretnamesi*, p. 71.

133. *Le Paradis*, p. 158; *Sefaretname-i Fransa*, p. 172. This trip is also mentioned
in *Le Mercure*, of June and July 1721, part I, p. 110.

134. This spatial construction was a new development. Glass window panes
which originated in Venice were a sixteenth- and seventeenth-century luxury.
The manufacture of glass panes became widespread in England during the eighteenth century because of the coal-firing technique. Braudel, *The Structures*, p.
183.

135. The term he uses is *tesavir-i acibe*. *Le Paradis*, p. 112; *Sefaretname-i Fransa*, p. 144.

136. *Le Paradis*, pp. 132–134; *Sefaretname-i Fransa*, p. 159.

137. *Le Paradis*, p. 164; *Sefaretname-i Fransa*, p. 176; *Mehmed Efendi'nin Sefaretnamesi*, p. 58.

138. Adıvar, *Osmanlı*, p. 105; Akdeniz, *Osmanlılarda*, p. 63.

139. Akdeniz, *Osmanlılarda*, p. 63.

140. *Le Paradis*, pp. 108–109; *Sefaretname-i Fransa*, pp. 140–141; *Mehmed Efendi'nin Sefaretnamesi*, p. 37.

141. *Le Paradis*, pp. 114–115; *Sefaretname-i Fransa*, pp. 145–146; *Mehmed Efendi'nin Sefaretnamesi*, pp. 41–42.

142. *Le Paradis*, pp. 109–110; *Sefaretname-i Fransa*, p. 142; *Mehmed Efendi'nin Sefaretnamesi*, p. 43.

143. *Le Paradis*, pp. 147–153; *Sefaretname-i Fransa*, pp. 165–168; *Mehmed Efendi'nin Sefaretnamesi*, pp. 65–67.

144. *Le Paradis*, pp. 150–151; *Sefaretname-i Fransa*, pp. 159–160; *Mehmed Efendi'nin Sefaretnamesi*, 64. The French accounts also mention the visit to the observatory; *Le Mercure*, of June and July 1721, p. 112.

145. *Le Paradis*, pp. 131–132; *Sefaretname-i Fransa*, pp. 157–158; *Mehmed Efendi'nin Sefaretnamesi*, pp. 54–56.

146. Akıncı, *Türk-Fransız*, p. 16.

147. Balleroy, *Les Correspondants*, p. 343; *Le Mercure* of June and July 1721, part I, p. 124.

148. Buvat, *Journal*, p. 269; *Le Mercure* of April 1721, pp. 166–167, states that Mehmed Efendi presented a manuscript of Planude on the Greek translation of Boece.

149. Saint-Simon, *Memoires*, p. 202.

150. *Encyclopedia of Islam*, "Hiba" article, p. 343.

151. See Appendix D for the lists of the gifts given by Mehmed Efendi to the King and the Regent; of the King to Mehmed Efendi, his son, and the rest of his retinue; compared with the gifts given by Mehmed Said Efendi to the King; of the King to Mehmed Said Efendi.

152. The latter was the customary gift, d'Aubigny, "Un Ambassadeur," p. 22.

Chapter 3

1. Bonnac's remarks on the embassy, cited in *Le Paradis*, p. 236.

2. *Le Mercure* of May 1721, p. 145; *Nouvelle Description*, p. 258.

3. *Le Mercure* of June and July 1721, part I, p. 124.

4. *Nouvelle Description*, pp. 263–264, states "some Muslims in his retinue, seeing the examples of piety (in France) embraced our religion."

5. d'Aubigny, "Un Ambassadeur," p. 223. The "attendant" was most probably the personal physician of Mehmed Efendi.

6. Desmet-Grégoire, *Le Divan*, pp. 41–42.

7. *Nouvelle Description*, p. 264.

8. d'Aubigny, "Un Ambassadeur," p. 223.

9. Gasté, "Retour," p. 78.

10. Ibid., p. 81.

11. *Le Paradis,* p. 229.

12. Hattox in *Coffee and Coffeehouses,* pp. 11–27, traces the origins of coffee in the Near East. According to his account, coffee originated in Ethiopia and was used in Yemen. Traders and travelers brought coffee into other areas of the Arabian peninsula. By the sixteenth century, coffee had spread from the Yemen to the Hijaz, Cairo, and Syria. It was carried to Istanbul later in the century. Braudel traces the use of coffee in Europe in *The Structures,* pp. 256–259. According to him, coffee reached Venice about 1615. A merchant, de La Roque, brought the first coffee beans to Marseilles in 1644. Coffee was first used as a drug; it became an item for popular public consumption "in 1669 when a Turkish ambassador who entertained a great deal offered coffee to his Parisian guests." (This ambassador was Müteferrika Süleyman Ağa who was sent as an Ottoman envoy to Louis XIV.) Coffee sellers and peddlers appeared on scene during the last years of the seventeenth century. Coffee shrubs around Mocha in Arabia were the sole source of coffee until the eighteenth century. They were then planted in Java from 1712, on Bourbon Island (Reunion) from 1716, on the Island of Cayenne from 1722, in Martinique from 1723–1730, and in Santo Domingo from 1731.

13. According to *Le Mercure,* of September 1721, pp. 214–216, Mehmed Efendi arrived in Lyon on the twentieth of August and visited the library of the Jesuits as well as silver and gold cloth manufacturers.

14. *Nouvelle Description,* p. 263.

15. Gasté, "Retour," p. 139.

16. *Le Paradis,* p. 37.

17. d'Aubigny, "Un Ambassadeur," p. 233.

18. Ibid., p. 235.

19. Unat, *Osmanlı Sefirleri,* p. 46.

20. *Le Paradis,* pp. 234–236.

21. Lewis, *Muslim Discovery,* p. 116.

22. Buvat, *Journal,* pp. 240–241.

23. Gasté, "Retour," p. 101.

24. d'Aubigny, "Un Ambassadeur," p. 83.

25. Shay, *The Ottoman Empire,* p. 88, in the report of 13 October 1721.

26. Ibid., p. 100, in the report of 23 March 1723.

27. Ahmet Refik, *Tarihi Simalar,* pp. 36–37.

28. d'Aubigny, "Un Ambassadeur," p. 212.

29. Lemontey, *Histoire,* p. 455.

30. Lemontey, *Histoire,* p. 456; Martin, *Histoire,* p. 104.

31. Martin, *Histoire,* p. 104.

32. d'Aubigny, "Un Ambassadeur," pp. 88–89; for comparison, see *Le Paradis,* pp. 139–146; *Sefaretname-i Fransa,* pp. 163–164.

33. *Le Paradis,* p. 103.

34. *Le Paradis,* pp. 142, 234–236. This is the first passage Bonnac deletes from

the account. This entire discussion on slaves with Dubois is not included in the Ottoman and Turkish texts.

35. Ibid., pp. 234–236.

36. On his way to France, Mehmed Efendi had indeed ransomed "a Captain Solyman for four-thousand piasters" on the island of Malta. *Nouvelle Description*, p. 217.

37. de Flassan, *Histoire*, pp. 488–494.

38. *Le Paradis*, p. 169.

39. Schefer, *Mémoire Historique*, p. xlv.

40. Gasté, "Retour," pp. 107–108.

41. Ibid., p. 110.

42. *Le Paradis*, pp. 234–236.

43. Ibid., p. 236.

44. Buvat, *Histoire*, p. 259; *Mercure de France*, June and July 1721, part I, p. 108. Monsieur d'Ozambrai was the Director General of the Postal Service and an honorary member of the Royal Academy of the Sciences.

45. Marais, *Journal*, p. 172.

46. Buvat, *Journal*, pp. 235–236; Balleroy, *Les Correspondants*, pp. 317–318.

47. *Memoires*, p. 202.

48. *Mercure de France*, of June and July 1721, part I, pp. 113–114.

49. Ibid., p. 113.

50. Süreyya, *Sicil*, vol. 4, p. 226; *Mufassal Osmanlı*, vol. 5, p. 2441.

51. See figure on page 70 for a later drawing of Mehmed Said Efendi.

52. d'Aubigny, "Un Ambassadeur," pp. 233–235.

53. *Le Mercure* of June and July 1721, part I, p. 112.

54. Balleroy, *Les Correspondants*, p. 334; *Le Mercure* of June and July 1721, part I, p. 112.

55. *Le Paradis*, p. 223.

56. *Le Mercure* of September 1721, pp. 214–216.

57. *Le Mercure* of October 1721, p. 210. The report is dated 7 September 1721.

Chapter 4

1. Tanpınar, *Ondokuzuncu Asır*, p. 9.

2. Meyer, "Turquerie," pp. 481, 488; Clark, *Oriental England*, pp. 20–25, 31–35, 39. The European sources of information on Asia until the seventeenth century are discussed in detail by D. F. Lach in *Asia in the Making of Europe* in three volumes.

3. The description of the mission is in Meyer, ibid., p. 482.

4. Meyer, "Turquerie," p. 475 and Clark, *Oriental England*, pp. 41ff. discuss the themes of the Ottoman palace and the harem in European plays throughout the eighteenth century. For the effect of the Ottomans on Europe in the earlier centuries, see Clarence D. Rouillard, *The Turk in French History, Thought, and Literature 1520–1660*, Paris 1938.

5. Meyer, "Turquerie," pp. 477–478.

6. See figure on page 74 for a sketch of her in her Ottoman costume. The sketch was found in Otto Kurz "Pictorial Records of Favart's comedy "Les Trois Sultanes,"" pp. 311–317 in Kurz, *Decorative Arts*.

7. Ibid., pp. 484–485.

8. Desmet-Grégoire, *Le Divan*, p. 23.

9. *Le Mercure* of April 1721, pp. 165–175, notes some of these engravings and paintings. M. Coypel presented the sketch on the twenty-eighth of March.

10. Ibid., p. 166.

11. H. İpekten and M. Özergin, "Sultan Ahmed III," vol. IX, pp. 145–146; vol. X, pp. 126, 137, 142, 144.

12. Ibid., vol. X, pp. 137–138.

13. Ibid., vol. XI, pp. 133, 146.

14. Ahmed Refik, "Sultan Ahmed Salis ve Damadı," p. 151.

15. For a description of the site, see Uzunçarşılı, *Osmanlı Tarihi*, p. 163.

16. See figure on page 76 for one of these engravings. I am grateful to Dr. Gül İrepoğlu of Istanbul University for bringing these engravings to my attention.

17. This engraving is located in the Topkapı Museum Library No. H1975. The Ottoman term is *gümüşden kemerler*.

18. The description is of the Bassin de Neptune. The engraving is located in the Topkapı Museum Library No. H1973. The Ottoman term is *sim-i servistan nümayan olur*.

19. Ibid., p. 163.

20. *Le Paradis*, p. 50.

21. Vitol, "From the History."

22. *Le Paradis*, Appendix.

23. Ahmed Refik, *Lale Devri*, p. 41.

24. Ibid., p. 163.

25. Shay, *The Ottoman Empire*, pp. 20–21; Ahmed Refik, "Sa'dabad," p. 210; Eldem, *Sa'dabad*, pp. 14–15.

26. Eldem, *Sa'dabad*, pp. 14–15, 19; Ahmed Refik, "Sa'dabad," p. 210.

27. Ahmed Refik, "Sa'dabad," p. 210. The couplet is *"mübarek ola Sultan Ahmed'e devlette sa'dabad"* in Ottoman. Sa'dabad was destroyed during the revolt of 1730 and was demolished entirely except for the residence of the Sultan. The chronicler Subhi stated that the rebels wanted to burn the site. The new Sultan did not approve of the idea; he said Christians would laugh at such an action (of Muslims burning down Muslim residences). Instead, he gave permission for the site to be torn down, hoping at least to save some of the construction. According to his decree, the owners of the residences had three days to destroy their own buildings. Yet, when the town-criers started announcing the decree, the rebels acted before the owners and immediately began tearing down the residences. They even destroyed the gardens built around it. For a detailed account of this event, refer to Eldem, *Sa'dabad*, p. 20.

28. See figure on page 78 for an engraving of Sa'dabad.

29. The description was printed in *Le Mercure* of June 1724, pp. 1251–1264. It was in the form of a letter from a M. de V. to M. de la R.

30. Ibid., pp. 1253–1254.

31. Ibid., p. 1251.
32. Ibid., pp. 1258–1259. This information is the only existing information on the residences.
33. Ibid., p. 1260.
34. Ahmed Refik, *Lale Devri*, p. 41.
35. Schefer, *Mémoire Historique*, pp. xlv–xlvi; *Le Paradis*, pp. 48–50.
36. Schefer, *Mémoire Historique*, p. xlvi.
37. Schefer, *Mémoire Historique*, p. xlvi.
38. *Le Paradis*, pp. 48–50.
39. Schefer, *Mémoire Historique*, p. xlvi.
40. Berkes, *Development*, pp. 35–36.
41. Süreyya, *Sicil*, vol. 3, pp. 29–30; Ahmed Refik, *Tarihi Simalar*, pp. 40–60. Desmet-Grégoire, *Le Divan*, pp. 23–24.
42. Berkes, *Development*, p. 194.
43. Desmet-Grégoire, *Le Divan*, pp. 23–24. See page 70 for this painting.
44. Danışmend, *Osmanlı Tarihi*, vol. 4, p. 38.
45. Süreyya, *Sicil*, vol. 3, pp. 29–30; Akıncı, *Türk-Fransız*, p. 41. Succeeding chapters contain an in-depth analysis of the Ottoman printing press as a technological product.
46. Uzunçarşılı, *Osmanlı Tarihi*, vol. 4, p. 158; Gerçek, *Türk Matbaacılığı;* Babinger, *Stambuler Buchwesen*.
47. Danışmend, *Izahlı Osmanlı*, p. 16.
48. Uzunçarşılı, *Osmanlı Tarihi*, vol. 4, p. 158.
49. Ibid., p. 159.

Chapter 5

1. For a detailed description of all these embassies, see Unat *Osmanlı Sefirleri*.
2. For information on the Austrian campaign, refer to Uzunçarşılı, *Osmanlı Tarihi*, vol. 3 part 1, pp. 411–423.
3. Uzunçarşılı, *Osmanlı Tarihi* vol. 4, part 2. See pp. 217–220 for an account of Ottoman-Swedish relations.
4. Unat, *Osmanlı Sefirleri*, pp. 70–71.
5. The original quotation is in *Tarih-i Raşid*. The quotation is cited by Berkes, *The Development of Secularism*, p. 33; Lewis, *The Emergence*, pp. 45–46; Lewis, *Muslim Discovery*, p. 240.
6. *Tarih-i Raşid*, vol. I, p. 125; *Silahdar Tarihi*, p. 409.
7. *Evliya Çelebi Seyahatnamesi*, vol. 7, pp. 105–196.
8. Hoci, "Sadr-ı azam Said Mehmed," pp. 658–659.
9. Kara Mehmed Paşa's translator was Meninski, the author of the famous Turkish-French dictionary. Unat, *Osmanlı Sefirleri*, p. 47.
10. *Evliya Çelebi Seyahatnamesi*, p. 121.
11. *Tarih-i Raşid*, p. 123; *Silahdar Tarihi*, p. 406.
12. *Evliya Çelebi Seyahatnamesi*, pp. 192–194.

13. *Tarih-i Raşid,* p. 125; *Silahdar Tarihi,* p. 408.

14. Each day, fifteen sheep, two lambs, seventy *keyl*s of barley, and sufficient hay and wood were provided along with a daily stipend to each of 150 guruş. These two accounts do not supply much information on Austrian society; Mehmed Paşa was culturally closed to Ottoman society.

15. Hoci, "Sadr-ı azam Said Mehmed," p. 664.

16. Ibid, p. 665.

17. Ibid., p. 666.

18. Ibid., p. 673.

19. Ibid., p. 674.

20. Said Efendi, who has been to Paris before, is able to compare European cities with one another.

21. Ibid., p. 675.

22. *Evliya Çelebi Seyahatnamesi,* pp. 83–84.

23. *Tarih-i Raşid,* p. 122; *Silahdar Tarihi,* p. 405.

24. *Evliya Çelebi Seyahatnamesi,* pp. 147–148.

25. See Gibb and Bowen, *Islamic Society and the West* for a discussion of these concepts.

26. Ibid., pp. 152–205.

27. Hoci, "Sadr-ı azam Said Mehmed," pp. 666–667.

28. *Evliya Çelebi Seyahatnamesi,* pp. 83–84.

29. Ibid., p. 104.

30. Ibid., p. 113. The slaves were Moslem slaves; Kara Mehmed Paşa received ten, while Evliya was given five.

31. Hoci, "Sadr-ı azam Said Mehmed," p. 661.

32. Ibid., p. 663.

33. Ibid., pp. 663–664.

34. Ibid., p. 667.

35. Uzunçarşılı, *Osmanlı Tarihi,* vol. 4, part 1, pp. 322–324.

36. Frengistan is a term used by the Ottomans to refer to the West in general. Its literal meaning is "the land of the Franks."

37. Ibid., p. 236.

38. Hoci, "Sadr-ı azam Mehmed Said," pp. 675–677.

Chapter 6

1. F. Masson, "Les Jeunes de Langues," p. 930.

2. Naff, "Ottoman Diplomatic," p. 91; Parry, *The Age of Reconnaissance,* p. 19.

3. Parry, *The Age of Reconnaissance,* p. 1.

4. Ibid., p. 19. The source of the quote is Bernal Diaz del Castillo (A. P. Maudsley, ed. & trans.), *The True History of the Conquest of New Spain,* London 1908.

5. Nahid Sırrı, "Şark-ı Karipteki," p. i:71.

6. Iorga, *Les Voyageurs,* p. 92; for brief accounts on each traveler see pp. 93–99. There are references in P. Masson, *Histoire,* pp. 214–215, as well.

7. Iorga, *Les Voyageurs,* p. 93.

8. Twenty-two of these manuscripts were in Persian, Arabic, and Turkish. Omont, *Missions,* pp. 1055–1057.

9. Iorga, *Les Voyageurs,* p. 94.

10. Ibid., p. 97.

11. P. Masson, *Histoire,* pp. 367–368.

12. Bağış, *Osmanlı Ticaretinde,* p. 11.

13. Ibid., pp. 472–508, discusses the French exports in detail.

14. P. Masson, *Histoire,* pp. 431–471, discusses the French imports in detail.

15. Ibid., see pp. 509–656 for the French expansion.

16. Ibid., p. 4; the French embassy correspondence was filled with such edicts.

17. Ibid., p. 44.

18. Ibid; pp. 138, 181.

19. F. Masson, "Les Jeunes de Langues," p. 907; *Mélanges Orientaux,* p. v, footnote.

20. Bağış, *Osmanlı Ticaretinde,* pp. 23–25, summarizes these various attempts.

21. F. Masson, "Les Jeunes de Langues," p. 908.

22. P. Masson, *Histoire,* p. 52.

23. F. Masson, "Les Jeunes de Langues," p. 907. The expenses of the Chamber in 1774 were 323,470 livres, of which 277,000 were spent for consuls, 6,820 for the chancellors and 39,650 for dragomans and for this project.

24. P. Masson, *Histoire,* p. 146.

25. Collège de Louis-le-Grand was started by the Jesuits in the sixteenth century. In 1705, there were ten students from the Ottoman Empire; seven were Greeks and three Armenians. F. Masson, "Les Jeunes de Langues," pp. 908–910. During the first half of the eighteenth century, French boys and sons of Levantines were also placed into the College to teach them Turkish and Arabic. This practice continued until the French Revolution.

26. Ibid., pp. 910, 913.

27. Deherain, "Les Jeunes," pp. 385–410.

28. *Mélanges Orientaux,* p. iv.

29. Bookseller Colombat obtained the privilege to print grammars and small dictionaries of Hebrew, Chaldaic, Arabic, Turkish, and Persian; his son was very skillful at engraving the "poinçons," or points, of these languages. Ibid., pp. 108–109.

30. Bağış, *Osmanlı Ticaretinde,* p. 11.

31. Naff, "Ottoman Diplomatic Relations," pp. 89, 95.

Chapter 7

1. Chiang, *Tides from the West,* New Haven 1947, p. 4; as quoted in Cipolla, *Guns, Sails, and Empires,* pp. 147–148.

2. See Cipolla, *Clocks; Guns, Sails, and Empires.*

3. Cipolla, *Clocks*, p. 89.

4. For a discussion of the Ottoman use of Western technology, see Lewis, *Muslim Discovery*, pp. 223–229; Adıvar, *Osmanlı Türklerinde İlim*.

5. Rozen, "The Invention of Eyeglasses," pp. 217–218.

6. The poem runs, "My two eyes now serve no purpose at all/ Unless with the aid of Frankish glasses they become four." Quoted in Lewis, *Muslim Discovery*, p. 234.

7. Lewis, *Muslim Discovery*, pp. 227–229.

8. The discussion on the spread of tobacco in Europe is based on Braudel, *The Structures*, pp. 260–265.

9. The discussion on the spread of tobacco is based on Birnbaum, "Vice Triumphant," pp. 21–27.

10. *Tarih-i Peçevi*, Istanbul 1864, vol. i, pp. 365–366. Cited by Birnbaum.

11. *Ravzat ül Ebrar*, Bulak 1832, p. 501. Cited by Birnbaum.

12. *Mizan ül Hakk*, Istanbul 1889, p. 40. Cited by Birnbaum.

13. In classical medicine, all diseases were thought to be the result of an imbalance in the proportion of the four complexions of the human body: cold, wet, hot, and dry.

14. Ahmed Refik, *Eski Istanbul*, Istanbul 1931, 36ff. Cited by Birnbaum.

15. Landes, *Revolution*, p. 7.

16. Ibid., p. 87.

17. Kurz, *European Clocks*, pp. 20–21.

18. Ibid., p. 22.

19. Ibid., p. 24.

20. Kurz, *European Clocks*, p. 32; Landes, *Revolution*, pp. 98–99.

21. Landes, *Revolution*, pp. 238–239.

22. Kurz, *European Clocks*, p. 73.

23. Cipolla, *Clocks*, p. 88.

24. Landes, *Revolution*, pp. 58–60.

25. Kurz, *European Clocks*, p. 49. The quotation is taken from Aydın Sayılı, *The Observatory in Islam*, New York 1981, pp. 291–292, who cites J. Hammer-Purgstall, *Geschichte des Osmanischen Reiches*, vol. 2, pp. 465–466, J. H. Mordtmann "Das Observatorium des Taqi ed-din zu Pera" in *Der Islam*, XIII(1923), p. 83, note, and A. Sayılı, " 'Ala al Din al Mansur's poems on the Istanbul observatory" in *Belleten*, XX(1956), pp. 435, 455–456, 481–482 as references.

26. See Barkan, "Istanbul Sarayları," pp. 1–380, for such registers.

27. Ibid., p. 48.

28. Murphey, "The Ottoman Attitude," p. 297 note 2.

29. Kurz, *European Clocks*, p. 49.

30. Ibid., pp. 54, 82.

31. When the French ambassador began to repatriate them after the revocation of the Edict of Nantes in 1685, the Ottomans came to the rescue of the watchmakers. Each Ottoman dignitary claimed one watchmaker as his personal watchmaker. The French government was forced to give in.

32. Ibid., p. 55.

33. Uzunçarşılı, *Osmanlı Tarihi*, vol. 4, part 2, pp. 569–570.

34. Shay, *The Ottoman Empire*, p. 69. The correspondence is dated 24 February 1730.

35. Iorga, *Les Voyageurs*, pp. 95–96.

36. Ahmed Refik, "Sultan Ahmed Salis' in Hayatına Dair," p. 230.

37. Ahmed Refik, *Hicri Onikinci*, pp. 84–85.

38. Ahmed Refik, "Sultan Ahmed Salis ve damadı," p. 152.

39. He was the Sultan's son-in-law and the Grand Vezir in 1714. He participated in the Ottoman campaign against Venice and died at the Austrian campaign in 1716. Uzunçarşılı, *Osmanlı Tarihi*, vol. 4, part I, pp. 88, 122.

40. Ahmed Refik, *Hicri Onikinci*, pp. 56–58.

41. Omont, *Missions*, vol. I, p. 466.

42. Gündüz, "İslam'da kitap," pp. 183, 187–191.

43. For these developments of printing in Arabic script in the West, see J. Pedersen, *The Arabic Book*, Princeton 1984.

44. Pedersen, *The Arabic Book*, pp. 132–133.

45. Efzaleddin, "Memalik-i Osmaniye'de," pp. 245–246.

46. Gerçek, *Türk Matbaacılığı*, p. 14.

47. The following account is based on three sources: *Encyclopedia Judaica*, Jerusalem 1971, vol. 13, pp. 1100–1109, A. M. Habermann's *Ha-Sefer ha-Ivri be-Hitpathuto* (The History of the Hebrew Book), Jerusalem 1971, pp. 101, 124–126, 146, and his *Perakim be-Toldoth ha-Madpissim ha-Ivrim we-Inyene Sefarim* (Studies in the History of Hebrew Printers and Books), Jerusalem 1978, pp. 76–89. I would like to thank Dr. Minna Rosen for bringing these sources to my attention and kindly translating the relevant information in the Hebrew sources.

48. Lewis, *Jews of Islam*, p. 131.

49. Gerçek, *Türk Matbaacılığı*, pp. 18–19.

50. Mystakidis, "Hükümet-i Osmaniye," p. 324.

51. Gerçek, *Türk Matbaacılığı*, pp. 19–21; Mystakidis, "Hükümet-i Osmaniye," p. 324.

52. Mystakidis, "Hükümet-i Osmaniye," p. 324. Gerçek questions the authenticity of this decree in his book *Türk Matbaacılığı*, p. 9. This decree contradicts the previous favorable Ottoman policy on printed books. It might just signify an attempt by the Ottoman state to bring all printing activities under state control.

53. Ahmed Refik, *Hicri Onikinci*, pp. 32–33.

54. European rulers and clergymen had long been discussing the effects of "seditious books" on religious matters. Cipolla, *Literacy and Development*, p. 66.

55. Uzunçarşılı, *Osmanlı Tarihi*, vol. 4, part 2, p. 514; Karaçon, "İbrahim," p. 183.

56. Gerçek, *Türk Matbaacılığı*, p. 37.

57. For a discussion of the establishment of the printing press in the Ottoman Empire, see Gerçek, *Türk Matbaacılığı*, Istanbul 1928; N. Berkes, *The Development of Secularism in Turkey*, Montreal 1964; F. Babinger, *Stambuler Buchwesen im 18 Jahrhundert*, Leipzig 1919.

58. Efzaleddin, "Memalik-i Osmaniye," pp. 248–249; Gerçek, *Türk Matbaacılığı*, pp. 15–16.

59. Gerçek, *Türk Matbaacılığı,* p. 44.

60. Omont, *Missions,* pp. 394–399.

61. Pedersen, *The Arabic Book,* p. 134.

62. Gerçek, *Türk Matbaacılığı,* p. 48.

63. The two volumes together contained 1422 pages. Gerçek, *Türk Matbaacılığı,* p. 48.

64. Ibid., p. 49.

65. Ibid., p. 59; Omont, "Documents," p. 188.

66. Mystakidis, "Hükümet-i Osmaniye," pp. 325–326. He states the quote to be from H. Omont, *Missions Archeologiques Françaises en Orient,* Paris 1902, vol. 4, p. 543.

67. Ahmed Refik, *Hicri Onikinci,* pp. 123–125.

68. Ibid., pp. 152–153.

69. Ibid., p. 168.

70. Gerçek, *Türk Matbaacılığı,* pp. 45, 47.

71. Gerçek, *Türk Matbaacılığı,* p. 43.

72. Uzunçarşılı, *Osmanlı Tarihi,* vol. 4, part 2, pp. 518–519. Even though paper was being produced in the Ottoman Empire since the sixteenth century, the scope and quality of this production had not been very high.

73. Ibid., pp. 518–519.

74. Karaçon, "İbrahim," pp. 154–155; the description of the paper factory continues on for several pages.

75. Ahmed Refik, *Hicri Onikinci,* pp. 159–160, 165–166.

Chapter 8

1. R. Murphey in *The Scope of Geography* discusses the importance of cities as centers of diffusion. See especially pp. 29, 33, 53–55, 232–234.

2. The information on the population of Constantinople is provided in the article "Istanbul," pp. 242–243 in *Encyclopedia of Islam* by H. İnalcık.

3. Ahmed Refik, *Hicri Onikinci,* pp. 121–123.

4. For the effects of cities on diffusion, see Hägerstrand, *Innovation Diffusion.*

5. Wirth discusses the importance of cities as centers of civilization in *On Cities and Social Life.*

6. Tursun Bey, *Tarih-i Ebu'l Feth,* p. 42.

7. R. Mantran, "Foreign Merchants," p. 128, in Braude and Lewis.

8. Ibid., p. 129.

9. For the transformation in French diplomatic representation, see P. Masson, *Histoire,* pp. 50, 71.

10. Teply, "Nemçe İmparatorlarının." The article is based on K. Teply, *Kaiseliche Gsandshaften ans Goldene Horn,* Stuttgart 1968.

11. Ibid., pp. 250–251.

12. Ibid., p. 251.

13. See figure on pages 120 and 121 for such a depiction.

14. Braude and Lewis, "Introduction," p. 5.

15. For a detailed discussion of the position of the Jews in the Ottoman Empire, see Lewis, *The Jews of Islam.*

16. R. Mantran, "Foreign Merchants," p. 130, in Braude and Lewis.

17. M. A. Epstein, "The Leadership of the Ottoman Jews," pp. 101, 111, in Braude and Lewis.

18. Barkan, "Istanbul Saraylarına ait," pp. 352, 362.

19. Lewis, *Jews of Islam*, p. 133.

20. Braude and Lewis, "Introduction," pp. 24–25.

21. R. Mantran, "Foreign Merchants," p. 133, in Braude and Lewis.

22. K. B. Bardakjian, "The Rise of the Armenian," pp. 89–99, in Braude and Lewis.

23. Lewis, *Emergence,* p. 62; Braude and Lewis, "Introduction," pp. 24–25.

24. R. Mantran, "Foreign Merchants," p. 130, in Braude and Lewis.

25. Braude and Lewis, "Introduction," pp. 24–25.

26. R. Mantran, "Foreign Merchant," p. 133, in Braude and Lewis.

27. Lewis, *Emergence,* p. 62.

28. Barkan, "İstanbul Saraylarına," pp. 308, 352.

29. Bağış, *Osmanlı Ticaretinde,* pp. 25–26.

30. Braude and Lewis, "Introduction," p. 28, in Braude and Lewis.

31. Bağış, *Osmanlı Ticaretinde,* p. 28.

32. Bağış, *Osmanlı Ticaretinde,* pp. 28–29.

33. Ibid., p. 33.

34. Ahmed Refik, *Hicri Onikinci,* pp. 188–189.

35. This anecdote is repeated by Braudel in *Structures,* p. 207. The quotation is from the first volume of de Tott's memoires, 1784 edition, p. 111.

36. Ahmed Refik, *Hicri Onikinci,* pp. 66–67.

37. Ibid., pp. 30–31.

38. Ibid., pp. 88–89.

39. Uzunçarşılı, *Osmanlı Tarihi,* vol. 4, part 2, pp. 60–61, 79, 87–97.

40. D. Cantemir, *The History of the Growth and Decay of the Ottoman Empire,* two parts, London 1734, 1737. The frequent footnotes in his work illuminate his life in Constantinople and his relations with the Ottoman dignitaries.

41. Constantin, "La réactualisation de l'Histoire," pp. 61–62.

42. Ibid., pp. 63–64.

43. Cantemir, *The History,* pp. 67, 105.

44. Ibid., p. 243.

45. Ibid., pp. 67, 105, 243.

46. For this description, see Ibid., pp. 91–93.

47. Ibid., p. 151.

48. Ibid., pp. 439–453.

49. Ibid., p. 164.

50. Ibid., p. 30.

51. Ibid., p. 300.

52. Ibid., pp. 361–362.

53. Dennis, "Distance and social interaction," pp. 237–250.

54. *Encyclopedia of Islam,* "Askari" by Lewis, p. 712; İnalcık, "Capital Formation," p. 97. The analysis of Ottoman statecraft and the military class has been developed by İnalcık in numerous articles, primarily "The Nature of Traditional Society" and "The Ottoman Economic Mind" and in his book, *The Ottoman Empire.*

55. R. Mantran, "Foreign Merchants," p. 134, in Braude and Lewis.

56. See Aktepe, "Damad İbrahim Paşa devrinde Laleye dair bir vesika," and "Damad İbrahim Paşa devrinde Lale."

57. Aktepe, "Laleye dair bir Vesika," p. 117.

58. Aktepe, "Laleye dair bir vesika," p. 90.

59. *Encyclopedia of Islam,* "Istanbul" by İnalcık, p. 236. For the description of such a residence in the eighteenth century, see Aktepe, "Onsekizinci," pp. 16–18.

60. I. M. Kunt, *Sancaktan Eyalete,* p. 97; R. A. Abou-el-Haj, "The Ottoman Vezir", p. 441.

61. Kunt, *Sancaktan Eyalete,* p. 99.

62. Uzunçarşılı, *Osmanlı Devletinin Merkez ve Bahriye Teşkilatı,* pp. 168–170. See Appendix E for a full description of his household.

63. Ibid., p. 171.

64. Ibid., p. 207.

65. Gibb and Bowen, *Islamic Society,* I:i, p. 151.

66. Kunt, *The Sultan's Servants,* p. 6.

67. Uzunçarşılı, *Osmanlı Devletinin Saray,* pp. 308–339, focus on the palace pages.

68. Uzunçarşılı, *Osmanlı Devletinin Saray,* p. 123; Kunt, *The Sultan's Servants,* p. 47.

69. Kunt, ibid., p. 47.

70. Kunt, ibid., p. 65; Abou-el-Haj, "The Ottoman Vezir," p. 438.

71. Abou-el-Haj, ibid., p. 438.

72. Ibid., p. 443.

73. Cantemir, *The History,* p. 414.

74. Ibid., p. 445.

75. Income deriving from these properties and their descriptions are cited when they are endowed to the wakf.

76. Aktepe, "Nevşehirli," p. 151.

77. These were large houses let out in apartments to Europeans in Ottoman cities. Smyrna was a very important port city. This particular house in Smyrna contained twelve rooms with a sofa and a kitchen on the top floor, and two cloth cellars, three dress cellars, and a shop on the ground floor.

78. The witnesses of this endowment reveal another sphere of communication between the Ottoman dignitaries. Admiral Mustafa Paşa, the Janissary ağa, ağa of the cavalry, and the steward were among the twenty-four Ottoman dignitaries who witnessed the formation of this endowment.

79. Aktepe, "Onsekizinci yüzyıl," p. 20.

80. The house consisted of seven rooms on the top floor, four rooms on the ground floor, a cellar, and a courtyard.

Appendix A

1. This bibliographic information is excerpted from Unat, *Osmanlı Sefirleri,* pp. 57–58. These four manuscripts are in Fatih-Millet Library No. 836, Topkapı Palace Library Manuscript Section No. 1432, Zühtübey Library No. 340, and Istanbul University Manuscript Collection No. 3232.

2. These six manuscripts are in Berlin Staatsbibl. No. 196, Gotha Landesbibl. No. 148, Uppsala Un.Bibl. No. 294, Paris Bibl. Nat. No. 1408, Vienna Nat. Bibl. No. 1098, and Vienna Kons.Akad. No. 280.

3. Mehmed Raşid, *Tarih-i Raşid* (1660–1721), volume 5, pp. 330–367.

4. *Sefaretname-i Fransa,* eser-i Mehmed Efendi, Matbaa-i İlmiye-i Osmaniye, Istanbul.

5. Yirmisekiz Mehmed Çelebi Mehmed Efendi, *Paris Sefaretnamesi,* Kitaphanei Ebüzziya Serisi, Matbaa-i Ebüzziya, Istanbul.

6. *Relation de l'Ambassade de Mehemet Effendi à la Cour de France en 1721,* écrite par lui-même et traduite du turc, Julien Galland, Paris.

7. The 1841 edition was titled *Mehmed Efendi'nin Sefaretnamesi,* Firmin Didot Frères, Paris, and the 1889 edition was *Elçi Mehmed Efendi'nin Takriri,* Imprimerie de Victor Goupy, Paris.

8. Mehmed Efendi, *Le Paradis des Infidèles: Relation de Yirmisekiz Çelebi Mehmed efendi, ambassadeur Ottoman en France sous la Régence, traduit de l'Ottoman par Julien Galland,* Paris. The editor was Gilles Veinstein.

9. The book is titled *Nouvelle Description de la Ville de Constantinople avec la Relation du Voyage de l'Ambassadeur dē la Porte Ottomane et de son Séjour à la Cour de France,* Paris 1721. The embassy account is related in pp. 213–264.

10. Istanbul University Library No. 724.

Appendix B

1. d'Aubigny, "Un Ambassadeur," p. 230; Buvat, *Journal,* pp. 218–219; *Nouvelle Description,* pp. 218–220.

2. This physician might have been "the Jewish attendant Moise," who is reported by d'Aubigny as having deserted Mehmed Efendi in Paris. See Chapter 4.

Appendix D

Sources: Buvat, *Journal,* pp. 229–230, 286; d'Aubigny, "Un Ambassadeur," pp. 205–206; Flassan, *Histoire,* p. 488; Desmet-Grégoire, *Le Divan,* p. 231; Schefer, *Mémoire Historique,* pp. xliv–xlv; Balleroy, *Les Correspondants,* p. 347; *Nouvelle Description,* p. 261.

Appendix E

1. İ. H. Uzunçarşılı, *Osmanlı Devletinin Merkez ve Bahriye Teşkilatı,* pp. 168–170.

BIBLIOGRAPHY

Abdülhak Adnan, *La Science chez les Turcs Ottomans*, Paris 1939.

Abou-el-Haj, Rifaat Ali, "The Ottoman *Vezir* and *Paşa* Households 1683–1703: A Preliminary Report," *Journal of American Oriental Society*, XCIV(1974)438–447.

Adıvar, Abdülhak Adnan, *Osmanlı Türklerinde İlim*, Istanbul 1943.

Ahmed Azmi, *Sefaretname*, Istanbul 1886.

Ahmed Refik, "Bin yüz otuz birde Viyana'ya Sefir İzamı," *Tarih-i Osmani Encümeni Mecmuası*, VII(1915)211–227.

Ahmed Refik, *Lale Devri*, Istanbul 1913.

Ahmed Refik, *Hicri Onikinci Asırda Istanbul Hayatı (1100–1200)*, Istanbul 1930.

Ahmed Refik, *Hicri Onüçüncü Asırda Istanbul Hayatı (1200–1255)*, Istanbul 1932.

Ahmed Refik, "Sa'dabad," *Yeni Mecmua*, I(1917)209–212.

Ahmed Refik, "Sultan Ahmed Salis ve Damadı," *Yeni Mecmua*, II(1918)149–153.

Ahmed Refik, "Sultan Ahmed Salis'in Hayatına Dair," *Yeni Mecmua*, II(1918)229–232.

Ahmed Refik, *Tarihi Simalar*, Istanbul 1913.

d'Aigrefeuille, Charles, *Histoire de la ville de Montpellier*, Montpellier 1877.

Akdeniz, Nil, *Osmanlılarda Hekim ve Hekimlik Ahlakı*, Istanbul 1977.

Akıncı, Gündüz, *Türk-Fransız Kültür İlişkileri (1071–1859)*, Ankara 1973.

Aktepe, M. Münir, "Damad İbrahim Paşa devrinde Lale," *Tarih Dergisi*, IV(1952)7:85–126; (1953)8:85–104; (1954)9:23–38.

Aktepe, M. Münir, "Damad İbrahim Paşa devrinde Laleye dair bir Vesika," *Türkiyat Mecmuası*, XI(1954)115–130.

Aktepe, M. Münir, "Damad İbrahim Paşa evkafına dair Vesikalar," *Tarih Dergisi*, XIII(1962–1963)17–26.

Aktepe, M. Münir, "Nevşehirli Damad İbrahim Paşa'ya aid İki Vakfiye," *Tarih Dergisi*, XI(1960)149–160.

Aktepe, M. Münir, "Onsekizinci yüzyıl vezirlerinden Kapdan-ı Derya Kaymak Mustafa Paşa'ya ait Vakfiyeler," *Vakıflar Dergisi*, VIII(1969)15–35.

And, Metin, *A History of Theatre and Popular Entertainment in Turkey*, Ankara 1963.

Archives Historiques du Département de la Gironde, "Chronique Bordelaise de 1638 à 1736," Paris-Bordeaux 1921.

d'Aubigny, E., "Un Ambassadeur Turc à Paris sous la Regence," *Revue d'histoire diplomatique*, III(1889)78–91, 200–235.

Babinger, F., *Stambuler Buchwesen im 18 Jahrhundert*, Leipzig 1919.

Bacqué-Grammont, J., and P. Dumont, eds., *Contributions à l'Histoire Economique et Sociale de l'Empire Ottoman*, Paris 1983.

Bağış, Ali İ., *Osmanlı Ticaretinde Gayrı Müslimler*, Ankara 1983.

Balleroy, Marquise de, *Les Correspondants de la Marquise de Balleroy*, Paris, 1883.

Barbier, E. J. François, *Journal Historique et Anecdotique de Règne de Louis XV*, Paris 1947.

Barkan, O. Lütfi, "İstanbul Saraylarına ait Muhasebe Defterleri," *Belgeler* (1979)1–380.

Berkes, Niyazi, *The Development of Secularism in Turkey*, Montreal 1964.

Birnbaum, E. "Vice Triumphant: The Spread of Coffee and Tobacco in Turkey," in *The Durham University Journal*, XLIX(1956)21–27.

Božič, Mileva, "Le Fonds Imprimé Turc de la Bibliothèque Nationale," *Revue de la Bibliothèque Nationale*, I(1981)8–16, 70–79.

Braude, B., and B. Lewis, eds., *Christians and Jews in the Ottoman Empire*, vol. 1, New York 1982.

Braudel, Fernand, *On History*, Chicago 1980.

Braudel, Fernand, *The Structures of Everyday Life: The Limits of the Possible*, New York 1981 edition.

Braudel, Fernand, *The Wheels of Commerce*, New York 1982 edition.

Buvat, Jean, *Journal de la Régence (1715–1723)*, Paris 1865.

Cantemir, Demetrius, *The History of the Growth and Decay of the Ottoman Empire*, 2 vols., London 1734, 1737.

Carswell, John, "From the Tulip to the Rose," pp. 328–335 in T. Naff and R. Owen, eds., *Studies in Eighteenth Century Islamic History*, Chicago 1977.

Cicourel, A., ed., *Cognitive Sociology: Language and Meaning in Social Interaction*, London 1973.

Cipolla, C., *Clocks and Culture 1300–1700*, London 1967.

Cipolla, C., *Guns, Sails, and Empires: Technological Innovation and the Early Phases of European Expansion 1400–1700*, New York 1965.

Clark, T. Blake, *Oriental England: A Study of Oriental Influences in Eighteenth Century England as reflected in the Drama*, Shangai 1939.

Constantin, Gh. I., "La réactualisation de l'Histoire de l'Empire Ottoman de Demetre Cantemir," *Cultura Turcica*, V–VII(1968–1790)55–66.

Danışmend, İsmail Hami, *Osmanlı Tarihi Kronolojisi*, Istanbul 1955.

Dehérain, Henri, "Les Jeunes de Langue à Constantinople sous le Premier Empire," *Revue de l'Histoire des Colonies Françaises*, XVI(1928)385–410.

Dennis, R. J., "Distance and Social Interaction in a Victorian City," *Journal of Historical Geography*, III(1977)237–250.

Desmet-Grégoire, Hélène, *Le Divan Magique: L'Orient turc en France au XVIIIe siècle*, Paris 1980.

Douglas, Mary, *Cultural Bias*, London 1978.

Douglas, Mary, *Essays in the Sociology of Perception*, London 1982.

Efzaleddin, "Memalik-i Osmaniye'de Taba'atin Kadimi," *Tarih-i Osmani Encümeni Mecmuası*, VII(1915)242–249.

Eldem, Sedad Hakkı, *Sa'dabad*, Istanbul.

Elias, Norbert, *The Court Society*, New York 1983 edition.

Elias, Norbert, *The History of Manners*, New York 1978 edition.

Encyclopedia of Islam (New Edition), "Ahmed III," "Askari," "Bakhshish," "Elči," "Hiba," "Huseyn Efendi, known as Hezarfenn," "Istanbul," "Khil'a," "Kahwa."

Eren, İsmail, "Rucer Yusuf Boskoviç' in 1762 tarihli Istanbul Lehistan Seyahatine ait Hatıra Defteri," *Tarih Dergisi*, XIII(1961)16:83–106; (1962–1963)17–18:191–218; XIV(1964)19:141–164.

Esad Efendi, *Teşrifat-ı Kadime*, Istanbul 1979 edition.

Evliya Çelebi, *Evliya Çelebi Seyahatnamesi*, Istanbul 1981.

Fındıklılı Mehmed Ağa, *Silahdar Tarihi*, Istanbul 1928.

de Flassan, M., *Histoire Generale et Raisonnée de la Diplomatie Française*, Paris 1811.

Gasté, Armand, "Retour à Constantinople de l'Ambassadeur Turc Méhémet Effendi: Journal de Bord du Chevalier de Camilly, Juillet 1721–Mai 1722," *Mémoires de l'Académie Nationale des Sciences, Arts et Belles-lettres de Caen*, (1902)4–141.

Gazette de France, 19 Octobre 1720: No. 42, 15 Mars 1721: No. 12, 29 Mars 1721: No. 15, 19 Juillet 1721: No. 31, 20 Decembre 1721: No. 53, 10 Janvier 1722: No. 2, 21 Mars 1722: No. 13.

Gerçek, S. Nüzhet, *Türk Matbaacılığı*, Istanbul 1928.

Gibb, E. J. W., *A History of Ottoman Poetry*, London 1905.

Gibb, H. A. R., and H. Bowen, *Islamic Society and the West*, London 1963 edition.

La Grande Encyclopedie, Librarie Larousse, Paris 1975 edition.

Gündüz, M., "İslam'da Kitap Sevgisi ve ilk Kütüphaneler," *Vakıflar Dergisi*, XI(1975)165–193.

Hägerstrand, Torsten, *Innovation Diffusion as a Spatial Process*, Chicago 1967.

Halsband, Robert, *The Life of Lady Mary Wortley Montagu*, Oxford 1956.

Hattox, Ralph S., *Coffee and Coffeehouses: The Origins of a Social Beverage in the Medieval Near East*, Seattle 1985.

Herbette, Maurice, *Une Ambassade Persane sous Louis XIV*, Paris 1907.

Hoci, İskender A., "Sadr-ı azam Said Mehmed Paşa merhumun hacegan-ı divan-ı hümayunda iken Istokholme vuku' bulan sefareti," *Tarih-i Osmani Encümeni Mecmuası*, I(1911)658–677.

İnalcık, Halil, "Capital Formation in the Ottoman Empire," *Journal of Economic History*, XIX(1969)97–140.

İnalcık, Halil, "The Nature of Traditional Society: Turkey," pp. 42–63 in R. E. Ward and D. Rustow, eds., *Political Modernization in Japan and Turkey*, Princeton 1964.

İnalcık, Halil, "The Ottoman Economic Mind and Aspects of the Ottoman Economy," pp. 207–218 in M. A. Cook, ed., *Studies in the Economic History of the Middle East,* London 1970.

İnalcık, Halil, "The Socio-Political Effects of the Diffusion of Fire-arms in the Middle East," pp. 195–217 in V. J. Parry and M. E. Yapp, eds., *War, Technology, and Society in the Middle East,* London 1975.

Iorga, N., *Les Voyageurs Français dans l'Orient Européen,* Paris 1928.

İpekten, H., and M. Özergin, "Sultan Ahmed III. devri hadiselerine aid Tarih Manzumeleri," *Tarih Dergisi,* IX(1958)134–150; X(1959)125–146.

İslam Ansiklopedisi, "Hil'at," "Elçi."

Itzkowitz, N., and Mote, M., trans. *Mübadele: An Ottoman-Russian Exchange of Ambassadors,* Chicago 1970.

İz, Fahir, *Eski Türk Edebiyatında Nesir,* Istanbul 1964.

Jarry, Madeleine, *Chinoiserie: Chinese Influence on European Decorative Art,* New York 1981.

Karaçon, Dr., "İbrahim Müteferrika," *Tarih-i Osmani Encümeni Mecmuası,* I(1911)178–190.

Keesing, R. M., "Theories of Culture," pp. 42–66 in R. W. Casson, ed., *Language, Culture, and Cognition,* New York 1981.

Kunt, Metin İ., *Sancaktan Eyalete: 1550–1650 arasında Osmanlı Ümerası ve İl İdaresi,* Istanbul 1978.

Kunt, Metin İ., *The Sultan's Servants: The Transformation of Ottoman Provincial Government, 1550–1650,* New York 1983.

Kuran, Ercümend, *Avrupa'da Osmanlı İkamet Elçiliklerinin Kuruluşu ve İlk Elçilerin Siyasi Faaliyetleri 1793–1821,* Ankara 1968.

Kurz, Otto, *The Decorative Arts of Europe and the Islamic East: Selected Studies,* London 1977.

Kurz, Otto, *European Clocks and Watches in the Near East,* London 1975.

Lach, Donald F., *Asia in the Making of Europe,* 3 vols., Chicago 1965, 1970.

Landes, David, *Revolution in Time: Clocks and the Making of the Modern World,* Cambridge 1983.

Leclercq, Dom H., *Histoire de la Régence pendant la Minorité de Louis XV,* Paris 1921.

Lemontey, P. E., *Histoire de la Régence et de la Minorité de Louis XV,* Paris 1832.

Lewis, Bernard, *The Emergence of Modern Turkey,* second edition, London 1968.

Lewis, Bernard, *The Jew of Islam,* Princeton 1984.

Lewis, Bernard, *The Muslim Discovery of Europe,* New York 1982.

Marais, Mathieu, *Journal et Mémoires de Mathieu Marais sur la Régence et la règne de Louis XV (1715–1737),* Paris 1864.

Marsh, Robert M., *The Mandarins: The Circulation of Elites in China, 1600–1900,* New York 1961.

Martin, Henri, *Histoire de la France,* Paris 1844.

Masson, F., "Les Jeunes de Langues: Notes sur l'éducation dans un établissement des jesuites au dix-huitième siècle," *Le Correspondant,* CXXIV(1881)905–930.

Masson, Paul, *Histoire du Commerce Français dans le Levant au dix-huitième siècle*, Paris 1911.

Mehmed Efendi, *Le Paradis des Infidèles: Relation de Yirmisekiz Çelebi Mehmed efendi, ambassadeur ottoman en France sous la Régence* (ed. G. Veinstein), Paris 1981.

Mehmed Efendi, *Sefaretname*, Constantinople 1866.

Mehemet Efendi, *Relation de l'Ambassade de Mehemet Efendi en France*, Paris 1841.

Mehmed Efendi, *Yirmisekiz Mehmed Çelebi'nin Fransa Sefaretnamesi* (abridged by Ş. Rado), Istanbul 1970.

Mehmed Raşid, *Tarih-i Raşid*, Istanbul 1865.

Mehmed Süreyya, *Sicil-i Osmani*, Istanbul 1890, 1893.

Mehmed Zeki, "Beç'de Osmanlı Sefiri," *Edebiyat-ı Umumiye Dergisi*, VI:325–329.

Melangés Orientaux, "Notice historique sur l'Ecole Special des Langues Orientales Vivants," pp. iii–lv, Paris 1883.

Mercure de France, Mars 1721, Avril 1721, Mai 1721, Juin et Juillet 1721 première partie, Juin et Juillet 1721 deuxième partie, Septembre 1721, Octobre 1721, Juin 1724.

Meyer, Eve R., "Turquerie and Eighteenth-Century Music," *Eighteenth Century Studies*, VII(1974)474–488.

Mufassal Osmanlı Tarihi, Istanbul 1962.

Mumford, Lewis, *The Culture of Cities*, New York 1938.

Murphey, Rhoades, "The Ottoman Attitude towards the Adoption of Western Technology: The Role of the Efrenci Technicians in Civil and Military Applications," pp. 287–298 in J. Bacqué-Grammont and P. Dumont, eds., *Contributions à l'Histoire Economique et Sociale de l'Empire Ottoman*, Paris 1983.

Murphey, Rhoades, *The Scope of Geography*, New York 1982.

Mystakidis, B. A., "Hükümet-i Osmaniye tarafından ilk tesis olunan matbaa ve bunun sirayeti," *Türk Tarih Encümeni Mecmuası*, I(1911)322–328, 451–458.

Naff, T., "Ottoman Diplomatic Relations with Europe in the Eighteenth Century: Patterns and Trends," pp. 88–107 in *Studies in Eighteenth Century Islamic History*, Illinois 1977.

Nahid Sırrı, "Şark-ı karipteki Fransız Seyyahları hakkında bir Eser," *Türk Tarih Encümeni Mecmuası*, I(1929)i:63–75, ii:49–71.

Nouvelle Description de la Ville de Constantinople, avec la Relation du Voyage de l'Ambassadeur de la Porte Ottomane, et Son Séjour à la Cour de France, Paris 1721.

d'Ohsson, M. de M., *Tableau Général de l'Empire Othman*, Paris 1791.

Omont, H., "Documents sur Les Jeunes de Langues et l'Imprimerie Orientale à Paris en 1719," *Bulletin de la Société de l'Histoire de Paris et de L'île de France*, XVII(1890)99–112.

Omont, H., "Documents sur l'Imprimerie à Constantinople au dix-huitième siècle," *Revue des Bibliotheques*, V(1895)185–200, 228–236.

Omont, H., *Missions Archéologiques Françaises en Orient aux dix-septième et dix-huitième siècles*, 2 vols., Paris 1902.

Orgun, Zarif, "Osmanlı İmparatorluğunda Name ve Hediye Getiren Elçilere Yapılan Merasim," *Tarih Vesikaları*, VI(1942)407–413.

Pakalın, Mehmet Zeki, *Osmanlı Tarih Deyimleri ve Terimleri Sözlüğü*, Istanbul 1954.

Parry, J. H., *The Age of Reconnaissance*, California 1981 edition.

Pedersen, J., *The Arabic Book*, Princeton 1984.

Pérès, Henri, *L'Espagne vue par les Voyageurs Musulmans de 1610 à 1930*, Paris 1937.

Porter, Sir James, *Observations on the Religion, Law, Government and Manners of the Turks*, London 1771.

Renda, Günsel, *Batılılaşma Döneminde Türk Resim Sanatı 1700–1850*, Ankara 1977.

Rozen, Edward, "The Invention of Eyeglasses" in *Journal of the History of Medicine and Allied Sciences*, XI(1956)i:13–46, ii:183–218.

Saint-Simon, *Mémoires de Saint-Simon* (ed. A. de Boisisle), Paris 1926.

Schefer, M. Charles, *Mémoire Historique sur Ambassade de France à Constantinople par le Marquis de Bonnac*, Paris 1894.

Shay, M. Lucille, *The Ottoman Empire from 1720 to 1734 as revealed in despatches of the Venetian Baili*, Illinois 1944.

Shaw, Stanford, *History of the Ottoman Empire and Modern Turkey*, 2 vols., London 1977 edition.

Spiridonakis, B. G., *Empire Ottoman: Inventaire des Mémoires et Documents aux Archives du Ministère des Affaires Etrangeres de France*, Thessaloniki 1973.

Tanpınar, Ahmet Hamdi, *Ondokuzuncu asır Türk Edebiyatı Tarihi*, Istanbul 1942.

Tanzimat, Ankara 1940.

Teply, Karl, "Nemçe İmparatorlarının Istanbul'a yolladığı Elçi Heyetleri ve bunların Kültür Tarihi bakımından Önemli Tarafları," *Tarih Araştırmaları Dergisi*, VII(1969)247–263.

Tunaya, Tarık Zafer, *Türkiye'nin Siyasal Hayatında Batılılaşma Hareketi*, Istanbul 1960.

Tursun Bey, *Tarih-i Ebü'l-Feth*, Istanbul 1977 edition.

Unat, Faik Reşit, "Ahmet III. Devrine ait bir Islahat Takriri," *Tarih Vesikaları*, I(1941)107–121.

Unat, Faik Reşit, *Osmanlı Sefirleri ve Sefaretnameleri*, Ankara 1968.

Uzunçarşılı, İsmail Hakkı *Osmanlı Devletinin Merkez ve Bahriye Teşkilatı*, Ankara 1984 edition.

Uzunçarşılı, İsmail Hakkı, *Osmanlı Devletinin Saray Teşkilatı*, Ankara 1984 edition.

Uzunçarşılı, İsmail Hakkı, *Osmanlı Tarihi*, vol. 3, part 1, Ankara 1983 edition; vol. 4, part 1, Ankara 1956; vol. 4, part 2, Ankara 1983 edition.

Vandal, Albert, *Un Ambassadeur Française en Orient sous Louis XV*, Paris 1887.

Vitol, A. V., "Iz istorii turetzko-frantzuzskikh svyazey posol'stvo Yirmisekiz Mekhmeda-Efendi vo Frantziyu v 1720–1721 gg." (From the History of Turco-French Relations: the Embassy of Yirmisekiz Chelebi Mehmed Efendi to France in the Years 1720–1721), *Narodui Azii Afriki*, IV(1976)123–128.

Weber, Max, *Economy and Society*, 2 vols., California 1978 edition.

Wharncliffe, L., ed., *The Letters and Works of Lady Mary Wortley Montagu*, London 1887.

Wirth, Louis, *On Cities and Social Life*, Chicago 1964.

Wortley Montagu, Lady Mary, *The Complete Letters of Lady Mary Wortley Montagu*, ed. by R. Halsband, Oxford 1965.

Wuthnow, Robert et al., eds., *Cultural Analysis*, London 1984.

INDEX